KATHERINE DUNHAM

KATHERINE DUNHAM

Jeannine Dominy

Senior Consulting Editor
Nathan Irvin Huggins
Director
W.E.B. Du Bois Institute for Afro-American Research
Harvard University

CHELSEA HOUSE PUBLISHERS
New York   Philadelphia

Chelsea House extends its thanks to Craig LeMay for his valuable
research assistance in the preparation of this book.

Chelsea House Publishers
Editor-in-Chief Remmel Nunn
Managing Editor Karyn Gullen Browne
Copy Chief Mark Rifkin
Picture Editor Adrian G. Allen
Art Director Maria Epes
Assistant Art Director Howard Brotman
Manufacturing Director Gerald Levine
Systems Manager Lindsey Ottman
Production Manager Joseph Romano
Production Coordinator Marie Claire Cebrián

Black Americans of Achievement
Senior Editor Richard Rennert

Staff for KATHERINE DUNHAM
Text Editor Marian W. Taylor
Copy Editor Ian Wilker
Editorial Assistant Michele Berezansky
Designer Ghila Krajzman
Picture Researcher Wendy Wills
Cover Illustration Gil Ashby, from a photo from the Belknap
Collection for the Performing Arts, University of Florida
Libraries

3 5 7 9 8 6 4 2

Library of Congress Cataloging-in-Publication Data
Dominy, Jeannine.
    Katherine Dunham: dancer and choreographer/by Jeannine Dominy.
    p.   cm.—(Black Americans of achievement)
Includes bibliographical references and index.
Summary: Studies the life and achievements of the black American
dancer and choreographer.
ISBN   0-7910-1123-2
            0-7910-1148-8 (pbk.)
1. Dunham, Katherine—Juvenile literature. 2. Dancers—United
States—Biography—Juvenile literature 3. Choreographers—United
States—Biography—Juvenile literature. 4. Afro-Americans—
Biography—Juvenile literature. [1. Dunham, Katherine. 2. Dancers.
3. Choreographers. 4. Afro-Americans—Biography.] I. Title. II.
Series.
GV1785.D82D66 1991   91-11276
792.8'028'092—dc20   CIP
[B]   AC

Frontispiece: *Barefoot and sporting
her trademark cigar, Katherine
Dunham performs in "Tropics," a
Caribbean-flavored dance she
choreographed in 1940.*

CONTENTS

BLACK AMERICANS OF ACHIEVEMENT

HANK AARON
baseball great

KAREEM ABDUL-JABBAR
basketball great

RALPH ABERNATHY
civil rights leader

ALVIN AILEY
choreographer

MUHAMMAD ALI
heavyweight champion

RICHARD ALLEN
*religious leader and
social activist*

MAYA ANGELOU
author

LOUIS ARMSTRONG
musician

ARTHUR ASHE
tennis great

JOSEPHINE BAKER
entertainer

JAMES BALDWIN
author

BENJAMIN BANNEKER
scientist and mathematician

AMIRI BARAKA
poet and playwright

COUNT BASIE
bandleader and composer

ROMARE BEARDEN
artist

JAMES BECKWOURTH
frontiersman

MARY MCLEOD BETHUNE
educator

JULIAN BOND
civil rights leader and politician

GWENDOLYN BROOKS
poet

JIM BROWN
football great

BLANCHE BRUCE
politician

RALPH BUNCHE
diplomat

STOKELY CARMICHAEL
civil rights leader

GEORGE WASHINGTON
CARVER
botanist

RAY CHARLES
musician

CHARLES CHESNUTT
author

JOHN COLTRANE
musician

BILL COSBY
entertainer

PAUL CUFFE
merchant and abolitionist

COUNTEE CULLEN
poet

ANGELA DAVIS
civil rights leader

BENJAMIN DAVIS, SR., AND
BENJAMIN DAVIS, JR.
military leaders

SAMMY DAVIS, JR.
entertainter

FATHER DIVINE
religious leader

FREDERICK DOUGLASS
abolitionist editor

CHARLES DREW
physician

W.E.B. DU BOIS
scholar and activist

PAUL LAURENCE DUNBAR
poet

KATHERINE DUNHAM
dancer and choreographer

DUKE ELLINGTON
bandleader and composer

RALPH ELLISON
author

JULIUS ERVING
basketball great

JAMES FARMER
civil rights leader

ELLA FITZGERALD
singer

MARCUS GARVEY
black nationalist leader

JOSH GIBSON
baseball great

DIZZY GILLESPIE
musician

CLARA MCBRIDE
("MOTHER") HALE
humanitarian

PRINCE HALL
social reformer

W. C. HANDY
father of the blues

WILLIAM HASTIE
educator and politician

MATTHEW HENSON
explorer

CHESTER HIMES
author

BILLIE HOLIDAY
singer

JOHN HOPE
educator

LENA HORNE
entertainer

LANGSTON HUGHES
poet

ZORA NEALE HURSTON
author

JESSE JACKSON
civil rights leader and politician

MICHAEL JACKSON
entertainer

JACK JOHNSON
heavyweight champion

JAMES WELDON JOHNSON
author

SCOTT JOPLIN
composer

BARBARA JORDAN
politician

CORETTA SCOTT KING
civil rights leader

MARTIN LUTHER KING, JR.
civil rights leader

SPIKE LEE
filmmaker

REGINALD LEWIS
entrepreneur

ALAIN LOCKE
scholar and educator

JOE LOUIS
heavyweight champion

RONALD MCNAIR
astronaut

MALCOLM X
militant black leader

THURGOOD MARSHALL
Supreme Court justice

TONI MORRISON
author

CONSTANCE BAKER MOTLEY
civil rights leader and judge

ELIJAH MUHAMMAD
religious leader

EDDIE MURPHY
entertainer

JESSE OWENS
champion athlete

SATCHEL PAIGE
baseball great

CHARLIE PARKER
musician

GORDON PARKS
photographer

ROSA PARKS
civil rights leader

SIDNEY POITIER
actor

ADAM CLAYTON
POWELL, JR.
political leader

COLIN POWELL
military leader

LEONTYNE PRICE
opera singer

A. PHILIP RANDOLPH
labor leader

PAUL ROBESON
singer and actor

JACKIE ROBINSON
baseball great

DIANA ROSS
entertainer

BILL RUSSELL
basketball great

JOHN RUSSWURM
publisher

SOJOURNER TRUTH
antislavery activist

HARRIET TUBMAN
antislavery activist

NAT TURNER
slave revolt leader

DENMARK VESEY
slave revolt leader

ALICE WALKER
author

MADAM C. J. WALKER
entrepreneur

BOOKER T. WASHINGTON
educator

IDA WELLS-BARNETT
civil rights leader

WALTER WHITE
civil rights leader

OPRAH WINFREY
entertainer

STEVIE WONDER
musician

RICHARD WRIGHT
author

ON
ACHIEVEMENT

Coretta Scott King

BEFORE YOU BEGIN this book, I hope you will ask yourself what the word *excellence* means to you. I think that it's a question we should all ask, and keep asking as we grow older and change. Because the truest answer to it should never change. When you think of excellence, perhaps you think of success at work; or of becoming wealthy; or meeting the right person, getting married, and having a good family life.

Those important goals are worth striving for, but there is a better way to look at excellence. As Martin Luther King, Jr., said in one of his last sermons, "I want you to be first in love. I want you to be first in moral excellence. I want you to be first in generosity. If you want to be important, wonderful. If you want to be great, wonderful. But recognize that he who is greatest among you shall be your servant."

My husband, Martin Luther King, Jr., knew that the true meaning of achievement is service. When I met him, in 1952, he was already ordained as a Baptist preacher and was working toward a doctoral degree at Boston University. I was studying at the New England Conservatory and dreamed of accomplishments in music. We married a year later, and after I graduated the following year we moved to Montgomery, Alabama. We didn't know it then, but our notions of achievement were about to undergo a dramatic change.

You may have read or heard about what happened next. What began with the boycott of a local bus line grew into a national movement, and by the time he was assassinated in 1968 my husband had fashioned a black movement powerful enough to shatter forever the practice of racial segregation. What you may not have read about is where he got his method for resisting injustice without compromising his religious beliefs.

He adopted the strategy of nonviolence from a man of a different race, who lived in a different country, and even practiced a different religion. The man was Mahatma Gandhi, the great leader of India, who devoted his life to serving humanity in the spirit of love and nonviolence. It was in these principles that Martin discovered his method for social reform. More than anything else, those two principles were the key to his achievements.

This book is about black Americans who served society through the excellence of their achievements. It forms a part of the rich history of black men and women in America—a history of stunning accomplishments in every field of human endeavor, from literature and art to science, industry, education, diplomacy, athletics, jurisprudence, even polar exploration.

Not all of the people in this history had the same ideals, but I think you will find something that all of them had in common. Like Martin Luther King, Jr., they all decided to become "drum majors" and serve humanity. In that principle—whether it was expressed in books, inventions, or song—they found something outside themselves to use as a goal and a guide. Something that showed them a way to serve others, instead of only living for themselves.

Reading the stories of these courageous men and women not only helps us discover the principles that we will use to guide our own lives but also teaches us about our black heritage and about America itself. It is crucial for us to know the heroes and heroines of our history and to realize that the price we paid in our struggle for equality in America was dear. But we must also understand that we have gotten as far as we have partly because America's democratic system and ideals made it possible.

We are still struggling with racism and prejudice. But the great men and women in this series are a tribute to the spirit of our democratic ideals and the system in which they have flourished. And that makes their stories special and worth knowing. ❧

1

"DO YOU MIND IF
I SHOW YOU?"

ON A WINTER'S day in Chicago in 1935, 25-year-old Katherine Dunham stepped nervously into a meeting room to confront a panel of stern-faced officials. Board members of a wealthy foundation called the Rosenwald Fund, these officials could help a deserving applicant pursue his or her field of study by awarding that person a substantial grant. Dunham, a university student and dancer who supported herself by working part-time as a librarian, understood that making a favorable impression on the board could change her life.

Unable to choose between her passionate love for dance and her growing interest in anthropology, Dunham wanted to find a way to pursue both. In truth, she believed them to be interdependent—that dance, a potent form of nonverbal communication, was as important to the study of human cultural history as language or architecture.

In the Chicago of 1935, it was no easy thing for a young black working woman to study dance or anthropology, let alone both. Dunham's father had achieved modest success with his dry-cleaning shop back in the Illinois town of Joliet, but he had neither the means nor the inclination to support his daughter

Katherine Dunham, 25 years old when she applied for a scholarship to study dance, had fallen in love with the art years earlier. "I was always thinking in terms of rhythm and motion," she said. "I danced because I had to."

11

in such impractical pursuits. Furthermore, the nation was in the midst of the Great Depression, the economic disaster that had overtaken it after the stock market crash of 1929. Unemployment was high, money scarce, racism worse than ever.

Racial prejudice had been bad enough before, particularly in the conservative and homogeneous Midwest, but it had intensified in the scramble for survival of the 1930s. Many whites were determined to grasp what was left of a badly damaged economy, and scholarship money was less likely than ever to fall to blacks.

In the world of nightclubs and theater, most audiences still thought of blacks only in terms of vaudeville shows or chorus lines with black—albeit strictly light-skinned black—show girls. Blacks were rarely viewed as serious dancers, nor was black cultural heritage something many people considered worth thinking about. Jazz may have swept the country and helped shape an era, but people thought of it simply as entertainment and did not much care where it came from. To most people, if this vibrant musical form was a black creation, its principal value lay in its appeal to white audiences.

Katherine Dunham had struggled to get herself into the University of Chicago and to keep herself there. She worked as a librarian, and to supplement her income and keep up with her dancing, she gave dance lessons. Her classes had led to recitals and shows for her students and to her own growing popularity as a performer in the Chicago area. Present at one of these shows had been an official of the Julius Rosenwald Fund.

The Rosenwald Fund had done much to brighten the otherwise bleak depression years in the Midwest. It had established the Museum of Science and Industry in Chicago in 1929 and had made large gifts to the University of Chicago. It had built 5,000 schools for black children in 15 southern states and given numerous fellowships for higher education. The fund was one of the few organizations that specialized in helping struggling artists, especially blacks.

Moved by one of Dunham's performances, Mrs. Alfred Rosenwald Stern had gone backstage to talk to her. She learned that the young dancer had developed some rather radical ideas about anthropology and dance and that she yearned to explore them. Dunham explained that she wanted to study the history of black dance—to find out how people had danced, why they danced as they did, what dreams and fears their dances expressed.

Without financial help, of course, Dunham could never make such a study. Intrigued, the Rosenwald executive suggested that the dancer ask for an appointment with the foundation's board of directors. She could present her arguments, outline her scholarly goals, and—perhaps—obtain a scholarship.

When the Rosenwald Fund set a date for her appearance, Dunham was terrified. She knew that countless needy students, most of them equipped with manuscripts and academic treatises to prove the merit of their ideas, came before the board every year. Dunham's ideas, although encouraged by her department head at the University of Chicago, were revolutionary to say the least, and by some standards, bordering on the farfetched. Few scholars had regarded dance as a cultural artifact, let alone proposed the formal study of tribal and—to the traditional American mind—wild and primitive dances.

Dunham, product of a hardworking family, had often wondered guiltily if she should give up her beloved dancing to pursue a strictly academic, "proper" course of study. And such a move might better demonstrate her gratitude for the university's generous

A 1939 publicity shot shows a polished and self-confident Dunham, a far cry from the nervous young dancer-librarian who had appeared before the Rosenwald board to win a dance-study fellowship in 1935.

support. But her heart and instincts told her otherwise, and she persisted with her ideas.

As the day of her board appearance grew closer, Dunham was haunted by questions. Should I present myself as an anthropologist first and dancer second or vice versa? she asked herself. Should I wear my best clothes or look truly in *need* of financial aid? Should I volunteer information or wait for their questions? How, indeed, could she convince the board that her theories had validity and thus gain its support?

When the fateful day arrived, Dunham donned her dance leotard, covered it with a neatly tailored suit, and set off for the fund's offices. Taking a deep breath, she entered the somber, menacing room of board members, educated people who heard more proposals and controlled more money than she dared to think about. She sat quietly and waited for them to tell her what they wanted to know. First, they asked for an outline of her thesis. She gave it quickly.

Then the board chairman asked, "What course of study would you pursue if you were given enough funds to explore your thesis?"

Suddenly, somehow, Dunham knew what to do. If dance was nonverbal communication, delivering the history and tradition of a people, why not go straight to the source? She looked calmly at the chairman and answered, "It's a bit difficult to put into words. Do you mind if I show you?"

The board members looked at her hard. At 5 feet 7 inches, she weighed 123 pounds, had pale brown skin, dark brown hair, and dark brown eyes—an attractive but not extraordinary young woman. Then she slipped off the suit and began to dance before the astonished board.

She performed a sequence of moves from classical ballet, followed by a series of familiar modern-dance steps. "That is what is being taught in Chicago and in most dancing schools of the country," she said.

As the board members watched intently, Dunham next demonstrated a polar opposite of the controlled, formal ballet she had just performed. She launched into a pulsating, hypnotic African tribal dance, involving her entire body from head to shoulders, from arms to rib cage, from hips to legs. The room was eerily silent, yet seemingly athrob with the insistent, ancient rhythm of an African drumbeat.

At the end, no one said much. Re-dressed in her street clothes, Dunham accepted the board's thanks, smiled politely, and left. Once more, she felt engulfed by questions and doubts: Suppose they thought my idea too experimental? Maybe my dance demonstration was too earthy. Maybe I should have talked more. Had her display, in short, worked for or against her? Certainly it was unprecedented.

Excited but frightened, Dunham spent the days that followed wondering what the board would say. Whatever their decision, it could well determine the course of her life. As it turned out, she need not have worried; as soon as the board members had recovered from her stunning "thesis," they had voted unanimously to give her a fellowship. They believed, as one said later, that Dunham "was on to something."

As Dunham had suspected it would, the grant changed the course of her life. Over the years, it would also lead to a revolution in American dance and to an exciting new awareness of black culture and history. ❧

2

"LOST IN THE WOODS"

Katherine Dunham was born in a Chicago hospital on June 22, 1909, and was brought to her family's two-story home in Glen Ellyn, a middle-class suburb of Chicago, nine days later. Glen Ellyn was "untouched at that time," she wrote in her memoir, *A Touch of Innocence*, "by the economic pressures or racial discriminations or restrictive codes of the city."

That had not been the case when her parents had moved to Glen Ellyn four years earlier. Blacks commuted from Chicago's congested South Side to work in Glen Ellyn as chauffeurs, gardeners, and maids. But very few of them lived in the suburban town.

Katherine's father, Albert Millard Dunham, had decided to move to Glen Ellyn shortly after he married the well-to-do Fanny June Guillaume Taylor, an assistant principal at a city school. Albert was an enterprising young tailor who had started his own business in Chicago with a friend, and he wanted his newborn son, Albert, Jr., to grow up outside the city. A wheat-field plot in the outlying area of Glen Ellyn seemed to be the ideal place to build a home.

His wife heartily approved of the site. Twenty years older than Albert and of French Canadian and American Indian ancestry, Fanny June Dunham had

Eight-year-old Katherine Dunham smiles from the back steps of her family's house in Joliet, Illinois, in 1917. Katherine's father, Albert, used the front part of the Bluff Street residence for his business, the West Side Cleaners and Dyers.

A 1905 photograph shows Katherine's mother, Fanny June Guillaume Taylor Dunham, cradling her son, Albert Dunham, Jr. Fanny June, who looked very young but was 20 years older than her husband, was of French Canadian and Native American ancestry.

five grown children from a previous marriage as well as four grandchildren, and she wanted to live in a house that was big enough to accommodate her large clan. She was also looking for an escape from the malicious gossips who had begun to point her out on the Chicago streets as a light-skinned woman who had married a black man.

But as soon as work began on the house in Glen Ellyn, the townspeople formed a committee to drive the family out of the area. First, a group of neighbors tried to force the Dunhams off their property for violating a local building code. When this action failed, someone tossed a bomb at the house. The blast shattered one of the downstairs windows but did little other damage; to make sure that nothing more happened, Albert spent every night for the next few weeks in a nearby toolshed with a double-barreled shotgun on his lap. By the time the house was finished, the Dunhams' neighbors had learned to keep their distance from Katherine's father.

Unaware of these incidents, young Katherine regarded her home as a happy haven, always filled with visitors and music. Every Sunday afternoon, her father entertained her with stories. At night, he played the guitar.

Whenever Albert, Sr., was not around, Albert, Jr., who was nearly four years older than Katherine, acted as her mentor. She recalled in her memoir (in which she always referred to herself as *Katherine* or *she*), "Her brother did not say much, but what he said was always wise, and she found herself listening more and more to his counsel and trying more and more to please him." In fact, as the years passed, the two remained so close, she said, that "the rising and setting of the sun would have been meaningless if her brother had not shared them with her."

In 1913, however, Katherine's seemingly secure world was turned upside down. One evening, she realized that her mother had not been home for several days. When Katherine wanted to know why, she was told her mother was very busy. Actually, Fanny June Dunham was seriously ill.

Katherine was getting ready for bed a few days later when she saw her mother standing in the doorway, wearing a snappy outfit. The four year old did not know it then, but her dying mother had tried to make herself look her very best because she had resolved that this was to going be the last time Katherine would see her alive. The next day, Fanny June confined herself to an upstairs room and refused to let the two children see the dreadful effects of the disease that finally took her life in January 1914.

Katherine's father struggled to keep the household together without his wife, but he did not manage very well. Fanny June's death seemed to take the spark out of him. He no longer played his guitar or told his children stories.

To make matters worse, he learned that his three stepdaughters had spent most of their mother's savings while she was dying, leaving him without enough money to pay for raising the two children. To help make ends meet, he put the house up for sale, gave his half of the tailoring business to his partner, and took a job as a traveling salesman. Before leaving town, he sent Katherine and Albert, Jr., to Chicago to live with their aunt Lulu Dunham, who worked as a beautician in the Fair Building, the same place that had housed his tailor shop.

Not yet old enough to attend school, Katherine spent most weekdays in Lulu's beauty parlor. On weekends, Lulu took the children to visit their grandfather and other relatives on their father's side of the family. A doting aunt, she worked hard to keep the children happy. Lulu, her niece recalled, "was fond of the children and they of her."

Yet their life in a cold-water, one-room apartment in the South Side slum known as Mecca Flats was not an easy one. According to Katherine, Aunt Lulu "lived in the City in what was virtually a tenement, and all sorts of odd people circulated around her just because she was goodhearted and unsuspecting and generous."

As 1914 wore on, it became especially difficult, even for someone as cheerful as Lulu, to retain a bright outlook. The number of southern blacks who migrated to Chicago in search of a better life increased daily, and the city's white population reacted with growing hostility to the black minority. For Lulu, the worst moment of this tense situation occurred when her landlord refused to renew her lease in the Fair Building.

In early 1915, Lulu tried to save some money by moving in with two cousins, Clara Dunham and her 17-year-old daughter, Irene. Amateur actresses, they lived in an apartment that doubled as a rehearsal space for a black vaudeville show they were producing. The singing and dancing that filled the apartment gave Katherine her first taste of the entertainment world.

Before long, the threesome of Lulu, Katherine, and Albert, Jr., was on the move again, this time taking up residence in a dingy two-room basement apartment with another cousin who went with Katherine to shows at the Monogram and the Grand theaters. The child carefully studied the performances of singers Bessie Smith and Ethel Waters, the dance

Katherine's stepmother, former schoolteacher Annette Poindexter, married Albert Dunham in 1917. Described by her stepdaughter as "fiercely loyal to the children," Annette quickly earned the affection of her new husband's motherless youngsters.

team Cole and Johnson, and the other entertainers. Especially delighted by the dancing, Katherine would attempt to show her brother the dance steps she had seen.

One day in early 1916, one of Katherine's half sisters, Fanny Weir, arrived at the basement apartment. She was, Katherine said later, "like some fairy godmother come to visit the babes lost in the woods and equip them with wings to fly to places of warmth and good food and pretty clothes." Piling the children into a taxicab, she took them to her comfortable home on the far South Side, "where a community of people neither white nor black," Katherine recalled, "but mostly passing for white, had penetrated beyond the barriers set up against their darker brethren." Thereafter, a court battle ensued over who would have custody of the two children.

The winner of the battle, as it turned out, was neither Fanny nor Lulu but Katherine's father. The two children were told to remain with their half sister until their father proved to the court he could provide for both of them. That day arrived the following winter, when word came that he had married a schoolteacher named Annette Poindexter and wanted his children to live with them in Joliet, a town about 40 miles southwest of Chicago.

Katherine and Albert, Jr., continued to live in different places during their first year with their father. They ate and slept in the back of his shop on Bluff Street, the West Side Cleaners and Dyers, then boarded with some local families before taking up residence once again in the rear of the clothes-cleaning shop. During the daylight hours, Katherine sewed name tags on the clothes to make sure they were returned to their proper owners. At night, she slept on a cot placed near the pressing irons.

Within a year, Katherine's father had earned enough money to purchase the carpet-cleaning busi-

Katherine takes the reins in Joliet. Her goat and cart belonged to a traveling photographer, one of many who recorded the lives of small-town America in the early 20th century.

ness in the same building, and the family moved into a large set of rooms on the second floor. Meanwhile, he bought a delivery truck and two recent inventions, an electric washer and dryer, to help out his growing business.

Sadly, this newfound prosperity did not bring Albert much peace of mind. According to his daughter, the pressures of proving he was capable of raising a family and running a successful business led to "patterns of anger, intolerance, and physical violence." Whenever either child stepped out of line, Albert reached for a leather belt strap to mete out their punishment. Most often, he took out his anger on his son, who was more interested in furthering his education than in working for the West Side Cleaners and Dyers.

Nevertheless, obedient and hardworking Albert, Jr., never let his studies get in the way of helping his father run the business. The youngster took care to do his schoolwork only late at night, after he had delivered the cleaned clothes and performed the many chores his father had given him. Even so, his father would insist that Albert, Jr., was wasting his time reading because he would be taking over the business someday.

By now it had become clear to the children that their father was not the same person who had once dazzled Fanny June Taylor. He would no longer take them on weekend outings; he could not afford to spend a single day away from his thriving business, he said. Determined never again to lose his family, he ruled it with an iron hand.

Katherine got along well with her stepmother, who was "fiercely loyal to the children" and "as full of mother love as a human being can be." But Annette Dunham was no match for her husband. Little by little, Albert's coldheartedness caused the family's bonds to unravel.

Katherine did not find her peers to be of much comfort. Most of the youngsters at the predominantly white schools she attended—the Beale School and the Farragut Elementary School—thought she was very shy and kept their distance from her.

At school, Katherine was an eager student who excelled in reading, composition, spelling, music, and physical education. Yet she had a difficult time measuring up to what she called her brother's "flawless record of scholarship." About to graduate first in his high school class, Albert, Jr., had set his sights on going to college. In fact, he had already begun to save every penny he had because he knew his father would never pay for his college education.

While her brother studied at every opportunity, Katherine began to widen her circle of friends and

Albert Dunham, Jr., sports an impeccable tuxedo for his high school graduation portrait. Katherine, who adored her big brother, said that without him "the rising and setting of the sun would have been meaningless."

At the age of 17, Katherine had already produced and starred in a successful revue—an evening of song and dance at the local African Methodist Episcopal church. Although she felt "like a prisoner awaiting sentence" before the show began, she brought down the house with her version of a Ukrainian folk dance.

become involved in a variety of activities. She began to take piano lessons when she was 11. That same year, she wrote a story that was published in the magazine *Child Life*. She also enjoyed putting on short plays with her friends.

By the time Katherine entered high school, she had grown to love sports as much as she loved performing. A gifted athlete who was tall for her age at five feet six inches, she became the starting center of the girl's basketball team and the track team's top high jumper. She was such a good athlete, in fact, that she was elected president of the Girl's Athletic Association.

Katherine soon added dance lessons to her growing list of activities by joining the school's Terpsichorean Club, which derived its name from the Greek muse of dancing and choral song. "I was always thinking in terms of rhythm and motion," she said later. "I danced because I had to."

Katherine's very first stage appearance was during a recital given by the Terpsichorean Club. She was assigned a minor role, however, and watched enviously as the star of the evening appeared in a pas de deux (a dance for two performers) and put on a wildly energetic display in the *gopak*, a Ukrainian folk dance. Vowing to learn the gopak, Katherine began to work harder than ever at her dance lessons.

Katherine saw a chance to showcase her budding talent when Brown's Chapel, the local African Methodist Episcopal church, sought a way to raise funds to build a new parish house. She volunteered to organize a cabaret performance with some of her schoolmates and charge the audience admission. Katherine herself would host the evening's festivities, dance in several numbers, including the gopak, and play the piano accompaniment to a vocal solo by her father.

As soon as the churchgoers approved the teenager's suggestion, the entire town began to buzz with excitement about the cabaret. Katherine's father arranged to rent the performance hall, which could hold 400 people. Her stepmother helped prepare the costumes. Some of the neighbors pitched in, too, including one woman who had starred in a black vaudeville troupe and possessed a trunk filled with theatrical gear.

Katherine ran herself so ragged preparing the cabaret that she developed a raging fever and lost her voice by the time of the final dress rehearsal. Unable to host the cabaret because she could not speak, the youngster was granted permission by her doctor to take part in just two performances: an Oriental dance and the gopak.

Waiting in the wings for her first number to begin, Katherine felt "more like a prisoner awaiting a sentence than the star of the evening," she recalled. As she began the Oriental dance, the stage fright that had taken firm hold of her would not loosen its grip. Performing before a packed house, she was so nervous that she forgot several parts of the routine.

Katherine's performance in the Ukrainian folk dance was a much different story. She leaped and twirled around the stage with so much nervous energy that the dance proved the hit of the evening. The audience called out for her to perform an encore, which she did, and presented her with a bouquet of flowers at the cabaret's end.

This triumph offered Katherine only a brief respite from her troubled home life. In the fall of 1924, her brother announced that he was leaving the local junior college he had just entered because he had been awarded a scholarship to attend the University of Chicago. Rather than celebrate his son's achievement, Katherine's father shut off all the electricity in the house that night to prevent Albert, Jr., from studying.

For Annette Dunham, this spiteful action was the last straw. Fed up with her selfish husband, she packed up her things and moved out of the house. The following morning, Katherine began to cry as she told her brother how upset she was at the thought of living alone with her father. He was a tyrant who would not even allow her to go out on a date.

As always, Albert, Jr., offered to lend a helping hand. "Say, Kitty, wouldn't you like to go to the University, too?" he asked.

"Yes," Katherine answered. "But it costs a lot, and I'd never get a scholarship."

"Never mind," Albert said. "By that time I'll be able to help you. Just keep going and don't pay any attention to him." He looked at her intently. "Don't give up, Kitty! Don't ever give up!" ❧

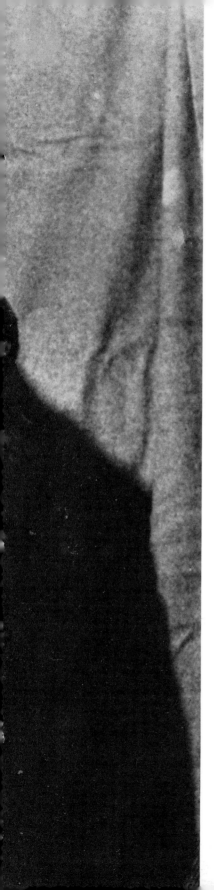

3

"TO FIND FREEDOM"

KATHERINE DUNHAM TOOK the first step toward independence from her domineering father on a cold March day in 1925, when she moved into a rented cottage with her stepmother. But not even the separation eased Albert Dunham's tight rein on his 16-year-old daughter. She and her stepmother were having a hard time making ends meet, and when her father offered an after-school job at his dry-cleaning store—where he could keep a close watch on her—she was forced to accept.

Katherine's long work hours grew even longer when Albert realized she was spending her brief free time with William Booker, a star player on her high school's football team: Albert gave his daughter so many chores that it became nearly impossible for her to do anything except go to school and work in the shop.

This situation continued well past the fall of 1926, when Katherine enrolled at a local junior college. Still eager to go on a date with her, Booker asked her father's permission to take Katherine out.

By the time she reached the age of 19, Dunham had attained her full growth: She was almost 5 feet 7 inches tall and weighed 123 pounds. Observers found her unusually attractive, but she regarded herself as "exceedingly plain" and considered her bosom too small, her hips too big, and her legs "not especially remarkable."

Not only did Albert Dunham flatly refuse, but he drove over to Elmwood Avenue, where Katherine lived, and hit his daughter for disobeying him. For the first time, Katherine fully understood that if she wanted to lead a life of her own, she would have to move away from her father.

The following year, Albert, Jr., offered his sister a chance to escape from Joliet. He sent her a job application from a Chicago library and an entrance examination for the University of Chicago. She filled out the application and took the test. Just before she graduated from junior college, the delighted young woman received two letters. The first, from Chicago's Hamilton Park Branch Public Library, informed her that she had been accepted as an assistant librarian; the second, from the University of Chicago, reported that she had earned top marks on the examination and was admitted to the college.

In her memoir, Dunham offers a verbal portrait of herself at this point. At the age of 19, she said, she "had reached her full growth of five feet, six and three-quarter inches, weighed one hundred and twenty-three pounds, and had dark brown eyes and dark brown hair, with a streak of auburn buried in the middle." Her skin, added Dunham, "was a light brown, so tinged with green that in strong light [it] might appear startlingly pale."

Still writing of herself as though she were another person, Dunham continued her critical self-description: "Her bosom was smaller than she would have chosen, and her hips were fuller. She had no high opinion of her legs, [regarding] them as useful objects, but not especially remarkable. . . . She found her features exceedingly plain and, because she had no hope of equaling her brother's scholastic brilliance, foresaw no exceptional future for herself. The most she could hope to do was find freedom. . . ."

In the spring of 1928, Katherine Dunham took a train to Chicago and moved into an apartment that her brother had found for her. A few days later, she headed excitedly to the library for her first day at work. "Her heart was in her mouth and her knees were weak," she wrote in *A Touch of Innocence*, "but she felt a great sense of elation, convinced that the most difficult hurdles of her life lay behind her. The past having been accomplished, the future could hold no terrors."

Nevertheless, she had to deal with a major problem right away. Chicago in the late 1920s was a fast-paced city that was home to more than 3 million people. Adding to the city's vast population was an influx of rural black southerners whose growing numbers contributed to increased racial tensions.

Dunham felt the sting of prejudice when she arrived for her first day of work: Bernadine and Blanche McLaughlin, the two elderly white women who headed the library, were visibly shocked when they realized the woman they had hired was black. They set Dunham to work cataloging books in a back room and assigned her to a lunch hour after the other employees had eaten.

That night, Dunham told her brother she wanted to quit the job. He managed to talk her out of it by reminding her she needed the income to pay her way through school.

When she began her first year at the university, Dunham was not sure what she wanted to study, but she knew she wanted to keep on dancing. Accordingly, she arranged to take both ballet and tap-dancing lessons. She also performed in dramas staged at the Cube Theatre, a small avant-garde playhouse her brother had helped to establish. Albert Dunham had completed his undergraduate education and was now working toward his master's degree.

Through these extracurricular activities, Katherine Dunham met several people who encouraged her to pursue a career in dancing. Chief among them was her ballet teacher, Madame Ludmila Speranzeva, who taught Dunham how to act out a story through dance. Speranzeva inspired the college student to dream of starting her own dance studio.

Dunham began to pursue this dream in earnest after her brother proposed marriage to her roommate and best friend, Frances Taylor. The couple moved east so Albert could study philosophy at Harvard University, leaving 21-year-old Katherine Dunham totally alone for the first time in her life. At this point, she decided to go ahead with her plan to open a dance studio.

At the Cube Theatre, she had befriended choreographer Ruth Page and ballet dancer Mark Turbyfill, both members of the Chicago Opera Company. When Dunham told them about her proposed school, the two artists responded with enthusiasm: Page offered to pay the rent for a studio on Chicago's South Side, and Turbyfill volunteered to work without pay as a dance instructor. Several students soon signed up for lessons; Dunham's career in the dance world had begun in earnest.

Normally a shy person, Dunham proved to be an assertive teacher, demanding that her students practice strict self-discipline and total dedication to their art. She was eager to experiment with new dance styles, especially the spirited movements she had seen performed by black entertainers while she was growing up. To identify her students as black dancers, she called her troupe the Ballet Nègre.

In 1931, Dunham's dancers received an exciting invitation. They were asked to appear at Chicago's annual Beaux Arts Ball, a showcase for young performers. The Dunham group staged "Negro Rhapsody," a dance number their teacher had choreo-

Dunham's friend Ruth Page appears in a 1934 version of Georges Bizet's 1875 opera, Carmen. A steadily employed dancer and choreographer, Page backed Dunham's first dance school, which opened in Chicago in 1931.

graphed especially for the occasion. It was politely received, but led to no offers of financial support for the school and no invitations to appear elsewhere.

Disappointed, many of the students left. Page and Turbyfill, unable to continue their contributions without the prospect of funds, also dropped out, leaving Dunham with only a handful of students, no studio, and no teacher but herself. She closed the school, but she continued to study with her mentor, Ludmila Speranzeva.

Chance attendance at a University of Chicago lecture started Dunham off on a whole new approach to dance. The lecturer, a cultural anthropologist (one who studies the customs and beliefs of humankind and its various subgroups) who specialized in Africa, had talked about the strong evidences of African culture in contemporary black America.

Although white masters had done their best to stamp out all traces of their slaves' heritage and old habits, said the anthropologist, many customs and practices had survived. Nurtured in secret by stubbornly individualistic field hands and house servants, African ways—tales, cooking methods, religious observances, and dances—had been handed down from one black generation to the next.

Dances! Dunham listened in fascination and growing excitement as she heard that the cakewalk, the lindy hop, and a number of other dances then popular in white America had been born in Africa, home of many of her ancestors.

Resolved to learn more about the musical movements of Africa and their influence on contemporary dance, she enrolled in several anthropology classes at the university. She soon discovered that while her teachers were knowledgeable about some aspects of African culture, they had little information about dance. Nevertheless, she began to incorporate in her own work what she did know of African dance with what she knew about classical dance.

Speranzeva, who found her pupil's ideas exciting, encouraged her to start another dance school, one where she could put her new concepts into practice. The older woman gave Dunham space in her own studio where she could conduct classes. Dunham soon announced the start of the Negro Dance Group, a title that reflected her approach more accurately than the French "Ballet Nègre." This time, however, she faced a new set of problems.

Ambitious middle-class blacks—the very people whose children Dunham hoped to enroll in her classes—wanted nothing to do with "Negro" culture. They wanted their offspring to have the best chance in life they could get, and in an America dominated by whites, that meant identifying with European, not African, culture. If the daughters of these upwardly striving black families attended dance school, it would be to learn classical ballet, not some "primitive" steps and rhythms. With too few students to justify the existence of a school, Dunham once again sadly shut down her operation.

This time, however, her cloud had a silver lining: Choreographer Ruth Page invited her young friend to dance the lead role in *La Guiablesse*, a new ballet Page had created that told the Caribbean folk story of a fatally seductive witch. Dunham, of course, accepted in a flash. Her opening-night performance at the Chicago Opera House proved a great success, garnering praise from newspaper dance critics and catching the attention of an executive of the Rosenwald Fund.

Created in 1917 by millionaire merchant and philanthropist Julius Rosenwald, the fund's official aim was to promote "the well-being of mankind." It directed much of its effort—and money—to aiding persecuted Jews in the Middle East and to improving black education in the United States. When Mrs. Alfred Rosenwald Stern, an administrator of her late father's foundation, saw Dunham dance, she was impressed. Learning of the young woman's dream—to trace the history of African-inspired dance—Stern suggested that she apply for a Rosenwald scholarship. Dunham did not need to be told twice.

During her interview with the fund's directors, Dunham set their heads spinning with her unexpected, highly theatrical presentation. She received her Rosenwald grant in February 1935. The stage was now set; the curtains would soon open to reveal a blazing new American star. ◗◗

4

THE CARIBBEAN: START OF A LIFELONG LOVE AFFAIR

❦

KATHERINE DUNHAM'S CARIBBEAN field experience started in Illinois. Members of the Rosenwald board recognized her talent and intelligence, but they knew she had no experience as a scientist or as a traveler; accordingly, they strongly advised her to take a crash course in field anthropology at Northwestern University before she headed south.

In the spring of 1935, the 25-year-old Dunham signed up to study with Northwestern University professor Melville Jean Herskovits. A pioneering anthropologist who later established the first department of African Studies in any American college, Dr. Herskovits had earned scholarly fame for his investigations of the folklore, religion, and economic systems of blacks in Africa and the New World.

The professor started Dunham's basic training by teaching her how to work in the field. She already knew that a people's dancing expressed many things in their lives and that to understand their dance she

Dunham's dance company, which she established soon after she returned from her Caribbean field trip, performs "Fantasie Nègre" in 1936. A chorus of drummers accompanied the piece, which Dunham based on a dance she learned in Haiti.

39

would need to know not only *how* but *why* they danced. This, in turn, meant learning about their religion, tribal history, superstitions, and customs.

Herskovits taught Dunham about living with and learning from strangers; how to appear concerned and attentive but never inquisitive, never shocked or horrified, no matter how "foreign" a custom might seem. To study a culture in its natural state, he said, an anthropologist must strike a delicate balance between being an observer and being a participant; accompanying but not intruding on the lives of those under study. Dunham must strive to be empathetic but not romantic; analytic but not cold.

Under Herskovits's tutoring, Dunham became acutely sensitized to the importance of body language, the gestures and mannerisms by which people unconsciously communicate. He also emphasized the need to respect other people's values, even when they seemed misplaced. West Indian countries, for example, observed a widely disparate double standard for the sexes: Women were required to be chaste, modest, and obedient, whereas men lived as they pleased.

Herskovits, who was white, speculated that Dunham's own skin color would be a major asset in her Caribbean research. He predicted—correctly, as it turned out—that her racial identity would give her entry to areas inaccessible to even the most experienced white anthropologists. He warned her, however, that she might be appalled by West Indian attitudes about race.

Caribbean cultures generally defined people and their value by the shade of their skin; the lightest blacks formed the elite. In their own context, light-skinned Haitians and other West Indians were often as bigoted about black skin as were many American whites. As a progressive, educated American black woman, said the professor, Dunham was bound to find such attitudes repugnant, but she must keep her feelings under tight wraps.

Her instructor taught Dunham how to use special photographic and recording devices and how to care for them in a humid tropical climate. Because her contract with the Rosenwald Fund required her to keep meticulous research records and to write reports on what she found, Herskovits also carefully trained her in research techniques.

To cap off his speedy introduction to fieldwork in the Caribbean, the professor prepared his pupil for basic survival: how and what to pack, what diseases to watch for and guard against, how to use snake-bite and first-aid kits, how to protect herself from illnesses caused by polluted water and unsanitary food.

Three months after he started his lessons, Herskovits packed the young woman off to her new world, equipping her with letters of introduction to various island officials and scholars whose assistance might come in handy. Dunham borrowed a friend's typewriter and, for the first time in her life, boarded a plane. She traveled first to Washington, D.C., to get her passport and to say good-bye to her brother, by then a philosophy professor at Howard University.

From the capital, Dunham went on to New York City and, also for the first time, boarded an ocean-going ship, a cargo vessel bound for the West Indies. She planned to concentrate on Jamaica and Haiti, Caribbean islands where, she had heard, dance was a particularly potent and ongoing force.

In Jamaica, the apprentice anthropologist headed for Accompong, a northeastern village where she hoped to make contact with members of a group known as Maroons. Brought from Africa as slaves by the Spanish, the Maroons escaped to the mountains after the British took Jamaica from Spain in 1655. Despite repeated efforts to recapture them, the fiercely independent Maroons (named for an ancient

Spanish word for mountaintop) successfully defended themselves for almost 200 years, until Jamaica ended slavery in 1838.

By the time of Dunham's 1935 visit, the Maroons had lived in relative isolation for almost three centuries. As a result, they retained many of their African traditions, unaffected by western ways. Herskovits,

With its paved streets, French shops, and arcaded sidewalks, the business district of Haiti's capital, Port-au-Prince (photographed in the early 1930s), exudes an air of prosperity. Within blocks, however, the illusion vanished; most of the city's dirt-poor residents lived in rubble-strewn shantytowns and competed for food with starving dogs.

who had once briefly visited the Maroons, believed they could provide Dunham with an excellent introduction to the study of African culture.

Dunham's first field trip, which she would describe in her 1946 book *Journey to Accompong*, began with a trek by mule up Jamaica's wild, steep Blue Mountains. Accompanied by a guide and interpreter

Herskovits had met on his earlier visit, she carefully picked her way up an almost vertical trail. On top of the mountain, she entered the Maroon village where she would spend the next six weeks living in a two-room hut.

The villagers, who seemed as curious about her as she was about them, provided her with a straw mat for sleeping and a bewildering array of highly spiced tropical food. Violently ill at first, she soon adapted to her new diet and started listening appreciatively to the folk tales and oral history of her hosts. What she wanted most to experience—the dancing of the Maroons—proved much more elusive.

After several weeks, Dunham's goal finally seemed in sight. Explaining that an evening of dance was about to take place on the "parade," a flat hilltop overlooking the village, the Maroons invited her to attend. Delighted at this evidence of trust, she watched as scores of people from several neighboring communities assembled and chose partners. Then, to her dismay, she saw the men and women line up on opposite sides of the field and begin a stylized version of a formal European quadrille.

As the evening wore on, however, things began to change. Rum flowed, the drummers' beat steadily intensified, and the sedate western quadrille gave way to a hip-swinging, seductively rhythmic dance unlike anything Dunham had ever seen. The men turned into acrobats, flipping themselves in aerial loops and making impossibly high jumps. Wearing only long, flower-printed skirts, the women strutted, swung, and spun in a display of unabashed sensuality.

Dunham the anthropologist watched the gyrating figures in fascination. Then Dunham the dancer took over. Unable to maintain her scientific detachment, she joined the Maroons, quickly picking up the free, energetic, and frankly suggestive movements of a dance called the Shay Shay. Here her training paid off. Under the openly admiring gaze of her hosts, she whirled through the intricate steps with a grace and skill few other anthropologists could hope to match.

The young American found herself enthralled not only by the dance but by the position of Maroon women in their society. The best, most sought after— and sexiest—partners were women in their sixties and seventies. The younger participants, clearly respecting the grace and fluidity of their grandmothers and great-grandmothers, competed among themselves to imitate them.

As the torchlight began to pale before the dawn, Dunham and the other young women found themselves too weary to move. But the grandmothers danced on. Showing no sign of fatigue, they were still pounding and whirling when Dunham crept off to bed at sunrise.

Thinking about it the next day, the anthropologist realized she had learned something important from this dance: It revealed a sharp difference between the attitudes of the Maroons and those of the West. Unlike Americans, who tended to worship youth and denigrate age, these people valued the old for their experience and skill, a carryover from their ancestral homeland and its frequently matriarchal structure.

Dunham continued to behave with the utmost courtesy, never taking obvious notes, asking personal questions, or staring at her hosts. As their trust in her increased, the Maroons relaxed in her company, even allowing her to witness ordinarily secret dances and rituals. She knew she had been fully accepted— and that she had achieved her first real success as an anthropologist—when the Maroons invited her to watch the Koromantee, a West African war-preparation dance.

Calculated to arouse aggressive feelings in its participants, the Koromantee called for the female

The weekly market draws buyers and sellers to a Haitian country town in 1935. Thrilled to be part of a majority for a change—most Haitians were black or of mixed racial ancestry—Dunham loved visiting the nation's out-of-the-way communities, where African ways were often still very much in evidence.

dancers to grab the men by the shoulders and shake them, then to wave rattles in their faces; the male dancers, in turn, brandished sticks and clubs at their invisible enemies.

The Maroons powered the Koromantee's insistent rhythms with the goombay drum, a square wooden instrument played with a flat beater. In later years, when Dunham performed an adaptation of this dance, she always accompanied it with the goombay drum she had made after her Jamaican trip. The Koromantee was a dance that satisfied her both as anthropologist and as artist: Reflecting and stimulating the emotions of a culture, it also provided a thrilling theatrical experience.

Ready for further revelations, Dunham moved on. From Jamaica, she headed east across the Caribbean to Haiti, the independent black nation that occupies one-third of the mountainous tropical island of Hispaniola. Haiti was the world's first black republic. The Haitians had expelled the French in 1804 and in 1934, the year before Dunham's arrival, managed to end a 19-year occupation by the U.S. Marines.

Haiti—its beautiful coastline, its wild green mountains, its people and their immense pride in their hard-won independence—captured Dunham's heart at once. At home, she was a member of a minority, but here she was part of an overwhelming majority. (Almost 95 percent of the population was, and still is, black or of mixed black-white ancestry.) Here, she surmised, blacks had taken charge of their fate and were running their own country; here blacks could believe in themselves. In the years to come, Dunham would return to Haiti again and again.

She soon realized, however, that for all its welcoming population and stunning natural beauty, Haiti had its dark side: It practiced its own form of racism, and its economy was one of the poorest on earth. Visiting Port-au-Prince, the country's teeming capital, Dunham found herself shrinking from the all-too-common sight of famished beggars, ragged children, and starving dogs.

Compared to the Iron Market, the city's most notorious slum, the ghettos of Chicago's South Side looked almost comfortable. Still, Dunham felt that the Haitian poor, especially those who lived on their own tiny plots in the countryside, had a sense of freedom unknown to most slum dwellers at home.

To the young American, almost as disturbing as the pervasive poverty was Haiti's rigid caste system, in which *mulattos* (people of mixed black and white ancestry) were the elite. The lighter a Haitian's skin, the more likely that he or she would prove wealthy and educated; the darker the skin, the lower the individual's social and economic class. So strong was the culture's belief in mulatto superiority that even if a black Haitian managed to acquire schooling and riches, that person had no hope of social acceptance by the elite.

Dunham found this racial coding difficult to tolerate, but as a visitor, she knew better than to criticize it. For the first part of her stay in Haiti, she lived in the Hotel Excelsior, one of the few safe places for a single, young, American woman to lodge in Port-au-Prince. Managing the inn were the light-skinned Rouzier sisters, a pair of first-class snobs who exemplified the people of Haiti's elite. The two women liked their young American guest and resolved to cure her of her strangly democratic behavior.

Armed with Herskovits's letters of introduction, Dunham had started meeting Haitians right away. One introduction led to another; she soon had scores of friends—of all shades. The hotel-keeping sisters expressed pleasure when Dunham entertained professionals, smiling graciously at the sight of white or mulatto doctors, lawyers, and government officals. But when they observed her in the company of Dumarsais Estimé, Dr. Jean Price-Mars, or Fred Alsop, the Rouziers shuddered and did their best to explain the facts of life, Haitian-society-style: Acceptable people are mulatto or white and preferably rich and well-educated. Dark-skinned people are, without exception, inferior and to be avoided.

Estimé, a leading member of the Chamber of Deputies (and later, from 1946 to 1950, president of Haiti), escorted Dunham along the leafy, elegant boulevards of upper-class Pétionville and through the twisted, refuse-strewn alleys of downtown Port-au-Prince. The company of the popular and well-known politician assured the young woman of a cordial reception wherever she went.

Price-Mars, who became Dunham's close friend, was both a skilled anthropologist and a political activist. The young American appreciated his explanations of Haiti's different classes and of their religion. And she was especially grateful when Price-

Mars introduced her to his friends from the country's interior, mountain peasants who retained many of their African ancestors' ways. Estimé and Price-Mars were, in short, cultured, sophisticated, knowledgeable men. To the everlasting horror of the sisters, however, they were both very black, an unforgivable sin.

The Rouziers considered another Dunham friend, garage mechanic Fred Alsop, a little better than Estimé and Price-Mars, but not much. Uneducated and practicing an unacceptably lower-class occupation, at least Alsop was English-born and white, which placed him—in the sisters' eyes—considerably above any Negro, no matter how scholarly, public-spirited, or wealthy.

Dunham (right) relaxes with an assortment of Haitian friends in 1935. Her companions (left to right) are: the mountain woman Cécile; a local physician known simply as Doc; and Fred Alsop, an English-born garage mechanic.

Of all the people she met and befriended in Haiti, none became closer to Dunham than Téoline, Cécile, and Dégrasse. Residents of a mountain village where life still resembled that of 17th-century Africa, the three women brought Dunham news of local births, weddings, deaths, and the religious ceremonies that accompanied each.

The innkeepers, of course, refused to allow the black peasant women to set foot in their hotel. When the trio came to town, they stood in front of the Excelsior and shouted for Dunham; to the chagrin of the Rouziers, the American woman would then rush out and hug her comrades. These women, who became Dunham's lifelong friends, grew so fond of Dunham and so eager to help her that they persuaded their neighbors to let her undergo an initiation ceremony into their Vodun religion, better known in the United States as Voodoo.

Dunham was delighted. She was determined to master the nation's dances, and as she later told an interviewer, "You can't know dances in Haiti without knowing the cult worship, because dance grows out of the demands of the gods." Then as now, the majority of Haiti's citizens were Roman Catholic. Except for the mulatto elite and a scattering of well-educated blacks, a majority of Haitians also practice the traditional folk religion of Voodoo.

People unfamiliar with the Caribbean's folkways often think of Voodoo as a bizarre cult of black magic, love potions, and lucky charms. In fact, however strange it may seem to foreign eyes, Voodoo is a genuine religion, involving communication with higher powers and unity with nature's forces. Voodoo is extremely complex, but basically, it centers on the *Gran Mèt*, the creator of the universe who delegates an assortment of powerful spirits (*loas*) to deal with humankind.

According to Voodoo belief, everything, from people to plants to the earth itself, is inhabited by a loa; in a Voodoo ceremony, which involves hours of drumming and dancing, participants aim at communicating with that loa. A person who does become possessed often falls into a hypnotic trance; fellow believers treat that person with great respect because he or she has achieved the goal of the Voodoo service.

Dunham would eventually adopt the Voodoo faith, but her first experience with it left her more shaken than exalted. Off in her friends' remote village, she spent three days huddled on the floor of a special hut with several other initiates, all of them spread with a paste of herbs, feathers, animal blood, and eggs. Allowed occasional toilet breaks and periodically given sacred food, the group prepared for

Dunham, who fell in love with Haiti and would return again and again, made friends with everyone from peasant farmers to urban professionals and politicians. Here she chats with future Haitian president Élie Lescot in 1939.

Wearing her own version of a Caribbean carnival gown, Dunham twirls through a number patterned after dances she had observed in Cap Haitien, a seaport in northern Haiti.

possession by a loa as, outside the hut, drums beat ceaselessly.

After the three days had passed, Dunham and the others emerged, donned white robes, and joined the dance that would unite them with their loas. Dunham, naturally fascinated with the dance, later reported that she did feel a union with her assigned spirit, the serpent god, Damballa. The spell broke, however, when she saw a boy bite off the head of a live chicken. Reverting to her unmystical, American self, Dunham raced off and vomited. Nevertheless, she saw the ritual through and received congratulations from her friends for becoming a genuine receiver of the Voodoo spirit.

Dunham, who recorded this and other experiences in her 1947 book *The Dances of Haiti*, regarded her introduction to the dancing of the Caribbean as the cornerstone of her career. After almost a year in the area, she returned to the United States in June 1936, endowed with sharpened research skills and the ability to blend in with and understand other cultures.

"From my own anthropological training," Dunham told an interviewer later, "I've learned that you practically have to put yourself into the skin of a person if you're going to claim to know anything about him or her. If I learned anything on my trip, it was that I couldn't come into a culture as a lady anthropologist who knew dance and leave with any real knowledge of that culture's dances." From that point on, she would return from her travels with new ideas, new means of expression, always seeking to learn more about the origins of dance and, even more important, about what it means to be human. ◖◗

5

"FIRST PIONEER OF THE NEGRO DANCE"

◆◆◆

WHEN KATHERINE DUNHAM returned to the United States in June 1936, she was afire with new ideas about the dances of the Caribbean and their African roots. She was determined to introduce them in her own country, but she knew she would have to reeducate the public first; most Americans, even black Americans, thought of African and Caribbean peoples as primitive and of "black dance" as tap or perhaps the popular jitterbug.

Before she could start that project, Dunham had obligations to fulfill. She diligently finished her reports for the Rosenwald Fund, then completed her undergraduate requirements, receiving her bachelor's degree in anthropology at the end of the summer of 1936. Pleased with her work and sure she would make a good anthropologist, Melville Herskovits, Dunham's mentor at Northwestern, urged her to apply for another fellowship, this time from the Rockefeller Foundation.

By now, Dunham knew exactly what she wanted, and it was not anthropology. Fascinated though she was by the subject, she valued it chiefly as a tool for

Dunham performs in "L'Ag'Ya," a folk ballet she choreographed and introduced in 1938. Based on a ritualized West Indian fighting dance, the fiery "L'Ag'Ya"—always among Dunham's personal favorites—became a classic part of her repertoire.

learning more about her chosen field, the dance. If she won the Rockefeller grant, she could get a master's degree and a good job teaching college-level anthropology. But Katherine Dunham was a dancer, not a teacher. Nevertheless, she felt indebted to Herskovits and obliged to honor his wishes.

Another factor influencing her was the Great Depression. Under the leadership of Democratic president Franklin D. Roosevelt, elected in 1932, the nation had started its painful recovery from the economic catastrophe, but in 1936, times were still hard. A college teaching post was a sure source of income; a career as a fledgling dancer was a long shot.

While she was agonizing over her future and awaiting word from the Rockefeller Foundation, Dunham returned to her dance group, which had continued to work under the direction of her teacher and friend Ludmila Speranzeva.

Dunham, whose work was admired by other aspiring dancers and choreographers, had begun to be much talked of in the dance world, even in far-off New York City. In the early spring of 1937, she received a surprise invitation: The Young Men's Hebrew Association (YMHA), an organization that made a point of encouraging and showcasing the arts, asked the Dunham Dancers to appear in its Manhattan auditorium.

Barely pausing long enough to say yes, Dunham and her troupe grabbed their costumes, borrowed two old cars, and headed east. In March, they presented a "Negro Dance Evening" at the Manhattan YMHA. Sophisticated New Yorkers cheered and applauded Dunham's newly choreographed West Indian dances, strengthening her conviction that dance was her life's mission.

On her return to Chicago, Dunham learned she had been awarded the Rockefeller grant. Now she realized she had to make the choice between dance and scholarship. Finally, to Herskovits's dismay—and her own sense of lingering guilt—she asked for a postponement of the fellowship and got a job with the Negro Federal Theater Project. The group, one of a number of similar programs sponsored by Roosevelt's New Deal to support and cultivate the arts, employed dancers, choreographers, playwrights, and actors to develop their own experimental theatrical productions.

The Federal Theater's Chicago unit introduced itself with an early 1938 recital entitled "Ballet Fèdre." Centerpiece of the evening was "L'Ag'Ya," a Dunham ballet based on West Indian fighting dances and set in a fishing village she had visited in 1935. Dunham took pains to make "L'Ag'Ya" as authentic as possible. She used the same dance movements she had watched in the Caribbean and costumed her performers in the fisherman's hats and flowered, full-skirted, many-petticoated dresses she had brought back from the islands. The piece, identified by one newspaper observer as "the fiery folk ballet with choreography by Katherine Dunham," proved the hit of the evening.

Soon after the "Ballet Fèdre," Dunham choreographed and, this time, starred in another ground-breaking piece, "Biguine." The dance tells the simple story of a young peasant woman who comes down from her mountain home to sell pineapples. Carrying her only pair of shoes, she dances along the road as she imagines what life will be like in the big city.

As performed by Dunham, the woman's movements were soft, seductive, and, at the same time, wistfully sad. Viewers were impressed with "Biguine" and its star, who, said one critic, was "born to be alone in center stage." These two dances, "Biguine" and the "Ballet Fèdre," marked the real beginning of Dunham's career as a major force in black American dance.

John Pratt exchanges a tender glance with his bride, Katherine Dunham. Few of their colleagues and relatives approved of the couple's interracial marriage, but Dunham and Pratt were too much in love to care. Their 1939 wedding proved the start of a long and successful union.

Dunham's connection with the Federal Theater Project brought her more than recognition as a dancer. Working with her was a handsome blue-eyed Canadian, John Pratt. Described by Dunham's good friend and biographer, Ruth Beckford, as "a soft-spoken, gentle man with a wit that made him interesting to be with," Pratt was also a gifted painter and designer of costumes and sets. Pratt, 4 years younger than the then 27-year-old Dunham, later told her he had been intrigued by her reputation long before he met her at the Chicago theater.

While Dunham was rehearsing "L'Ag'Ya," Pratt heard backstage rumors that the theater's project supervisor was planning to cancel it; knowing how much the ballet meant to Dunham, Pratt went to her apartment to discuss the matter. The pair plotted a successful strategy to save "L'Ag'Ya," a move that made them into firm allies.

From that point on, Dunham and Pratt spent an increasing amount of time together, and they soon

realized they were in love. Ignoring the raised eye-
brows of their colleagues—interracial couples were a
rare phenomenon in the America of the 1930s—they
announced their engagement and went to tell Dunham's parents the news.

Albert and Annette Dunham, now reconciled
and still living in Joliet, reacted to their daughter's
decision with horror. Annette in particular found the
idea of a white son-in-law shocking, but Katherine
stood her ground. If her parents refused to accept
Pratt as her future husband, she said, they could
expect no further visits from her. When Albert,
grown mellower with the years, recognized the depth
of his daughter's feelings for the talented young
Canadian, he changed his attitude, but his wife took
longer.

In July 1939, Dunham married Pratt in a quiet
ceremony in Mexico. Eventually, Pratt's charm and
tact triumphed over racial prejudice, and he and
Annette became close friends. Pratt, in fact, would
develop such a warm relationship with Annette that
he often stayed with her while Dunham toured with
her troupe; when the elderly Annette died in 1957
(her husband had preceded her in 1949), the one
family member at her bedside would be John Pratt.

Dunham and her new husband now decided to
work as a team. They would establish a regular
company of dancers; Katherine would choreograph
and also perform; John would design the sets and
costumes. After the enthusiastic public and critical
response to Dunham's first Caribbean-inspired folk
ballets, the couple felt confident. They hired a
theatrical manager and prepared to show America
what black dance was all about.

The Dunham Dance Company's repertoire reflected a broad field: popular, contemporary black
dances; so-called modern dance; Caribbean and
South American native dances; re-created African

dance. Until this point, black dancers had generally tried to mimic traditional white troupes; Dunham's dancers celebrated their own unique heritage.

"The full cultural depth of the nation's largest racial minority," noted author Robert Coe in his 1985 book *Dance in America*, "remained largely untapped until a young University of Chicago–trained anthropologist named Katherine Dunham began her careful explorations into the origins of black dance in the Americas."

Soon after Dunham formed her new dance company, she noticed a newspaper advertisement: The great Duke Ellington and his orchestra would soon open at the Panther Room, a supper club in Chicago's posh Sherman Hotel. Hoping to introduce her group with a splash, the choreographer approached the club manager and said she would like to appear on the bill with Ellington. The manager seemed interested until he learned that Dunham's routine involved barefoot dancers. Never! said the manager. His elegant patrons would be horrified by the sight of bare black feet.

Dunham (center) and her troupe give Chicagoans a taste of the Caribbean. Shocked by the uninhibited performance at first, sedate supper-club patrons got caught up in the show and wound up stamping their feet and drumming on the tables.

Dunham, who wanted the work, got a flash of inspiration. The dancers' feet, she said hastily, would not really be *bare*; they would be carefully covered with makeup and painted with toe straps to resemble thonged sandals. Still slightly suspicious, the manager signed them on, an act for which he later congratulated himself: The group was a smash hit, garnering rave reviews and turnaway business. And his cherished patrons never even noticed that the performers danced "Rara Tonga" and "Bolero" in unmistakably naked feet.

The success of the nightclub show was satisfying, but Dunham yearned to take her company to New York City, then as now the dance capital of America. She got her chance in the fall of 1939. New York Labor Stage company director Louis Schaeffer, who had seen Dunham dance at the YMHA two years earlier, offered her the job of dance director for *Pins and Needles*, a new show about unions and the garment business. She accepted in a flash, planning to present her own company with the money she made from the musical. With her husband and 10 members of her dance company, Dunham moved to New York.

While she was staging the dance numbers for *Pins and Needles*, Dunham also rehearsed her troupe. For its Broadway debut, she choreographed a group of new dances that included "Tropics," set in Panama and featuring herself, complete with the immense cigar that would become her trademark; an American folk ballet, "Br'er Rabbit and de Tah Baby"; and a suite entitled "Le Jazz Hot," which featured the lively "Florida Swamp Shimmy." Pratt designed the costumes and sets for the show, called *Tropics and Le Jazz Hot: From Haiti to Harlem*. To unveil it, Dunham engaged Broadway's Windsor Theater for one night, Sunday, February 18, 1940.

With dancer Rex Ingram, Dunham appears as slinky, streetwise Georgia Brown in Cabin in the Sky. *Also starring singer Ethel Waters, the musical opened on Broadway in 1940, played five sold-out months, then embarked on a successful cross-country tour. A movie version of* Cabin in the Sky *appeared in 1943.*

That evening made American dance history. "Katherine Dunham flared into unsuspecting New York last night like a comet," wrote one newspaper critic the next day. "Unknown before her debut," he added, "she is today one of the most talked-about dancers." Dunham, said another observer, "appeared to draw her rhythms from the center of a volcano." And the prestigious *New York Herald Tribune* reported, "Last night Katherine Dunham broke the bonds that have chained the dancing Negro to . . . the white race and introduced us to a dance worthy of her own people. Miss Dunham is the first pioneer of the Negro dance."

Also winning high praise were Pratt's vivid, stylish costumes, "as brightly colored as tropical birds," according to the *New York Times*. A few viewers objected to some of Dunham's more frankly sexual dances, particularly the hip-swinging "Florida Swamp Shimmy." This number, sniffed one critic, was "markedly uninhibited" and "lacked restraint." Such remarks left the choreographer unruffled. "African movement is pelvic movement," she said, "just as movement in the head, arms, and upper torso is East Indian. It is natural and unselfconscious to the blacks."

When *Tropics and Le Jazz Hot* found itself swamped with would-be ticket buyers, Dunham happily extended the show's run, playing for another 13 Sundays. The presentation led to an exciting offer: a collaboration with the celebrated white choreographer George Balanchine in *Cabin in the Sky*, a new, all-black Broadway musical.

The show, which starred the incomparable singing actress Ethel Waters, also featured the Dunham Dancers and the choreographer herself as a tough but seductive character named Georgia Brown. Opening to more rave reviews, *Cabin* played five standing-room-only months on Broadway, then embarked on a cross-country tour.

The high point of the *Cabin* run came to Dunham in Chicago, where Melville Herskovits saw the show. Dunham knew how disappointed her old mentor had been when she opted for dance over anthropology, and she had always regretted hurting him. The day after he saw her dance in *Cabin*, he sent her a letter.

"I think you were very wise to concentrate on your dancing," wrote Herskovits, "and while it may have been nice to have you here I feel you are taking by far the better course." For Dunham, who found herself laughing and crying at the same time, these words meant more than all the cheers and bouquets that had greeted her performance.

When the musical completed its run in California, the dancer and her company moved on to Hollywood, where Warner Brothers had invited them to make a short Technicolor film, *Carnival of Rhythm*. The movie, which featured an all-Brazilian selection of song and dance, was in midproduction when a group of well-dressed men appeared on the set.

Dunham soon discovered that the visitors were Brazilian diplomats, alerted to the production by a call from a prominent local socialite. "Are you going to let these *colored people* represent Brazil?" the society woman had demanded. The potential crisis fizzled when the diplomats—like many Brazilians, of mixed racial backgrounds—watched the dancers in action, then warmly congratulated Warner Brothers for choosing the "Senhorita Dunham divina" to interpret their culture. The reaction of the wealthy bigot is unrecorded.

Dunham's 1940 arrival in the film capital coincided with its newly discovered passion for blacks. Suddenly hot were such stars as bandleaders Duke Ellington and Cab Calloway, singers Lena Horne and Ethel Waters, and dancers Bill "Bojangles" Robinson

Dunham (right) leads her troupe through a series of warm-up exercises before a rehearsal. Dancers often complained about the strict discipline she imposed, but most jumped at any chance to work with her.

and Bert Williams. Katherine Dunham, supremely theatrical to start with, turned out to be highly photogenic as well. She was also in the right place at the right time. Her movie career took off.

Dunham's film credits would include a movie version of *Cabin in the Sky*, again starring Ethel Waters; *Star Spangled Rhythm*, with comic Eddie "Rochester" Anderson; *Stormy Weather*, with Lena Horne and Bojangles Robinson; and *Pardon My Sarong*, a farce starring comedians Bud Abbott and Lou Costello and set in Tahiti.

As the *Sarong* production got under way, its producer asked Dunham to design the film's big dance sequence, which he wanted authentic. He could offer her an unusually high fee, he said, because she was a known expert on Tahiti. Dunham, who had never been near the Pacific island in her life, realized the

Hollywood mogul had confused Haiti with Tahiti, but the money was too good to resist. "Well," she said, "you tell me the story and I can give you the type of choreography you need."

Signed contract in hand, Dunham headed for the public library and started poring over old copies of *National Geographic* magazine. After sketching an expensive set featuring a thick jungle and massive stone statues, she rounded up every dancer boasting even a hint of Samoan, Tahitian, or Hawaiian ancestry and went to work. When *Sarong* opened, reviewers heaped praise on its dramatic and "authentic" tribal dance scene. Ordinarily meticulous about authenticity, Dunham accepted the compliments with a perfectly straight face.

For a while, the choreographer and her husband enjoyed their large Hollywood house, their long walks on the beaches, and their growing bank account.

Costumed as usual by her husband, Dunham appears in Stormy Weather, *one of several movies she made in the 1940s. Also starring in the popular, all-black musical were singer Lena Horne and dancer Bill "Bojangles" Robinson.*

Still, as Dunham put it, "there was something phony" about the film capital; it also reeked of racial discrimination. Hollywood's "ideal black dancer," she wrote later, "was light-skinned, somebody who had danced at one of the famous whites-only nightclubs, like [Harlem's] Cotton Club."

Dunham, of course, never selected her dancers for their skin tone. "My company was what you might call a 'Third World Company' from the begining," she recalled. "We had Cubans, West Indians, Latin Americans, and their complexion didn't matter. What mattered was their talent."

In 1941, Dunham created a new show entitled *Tropical Review*, gathered up her dancers, and hit the road. The troupe gained wide acclaim as they toured the nation, but they also encountered more racial prejudice. In one city after another, finding sleeping accommodations and restaurants proved an exhausting struggle, but Dunham never gave in. Years after

Pardon My Sarong dancers perform the movie's big Tahitian dance scene, choreographed by Dunham. Aware that the film's producer mistakenly believed her an expert on Tahiti, Dunham cheerfully staged a phony but highly theatrical Pacific-island number, then basked in critical praise for its wonderful "authenticity."

it happened, she told the story of a night she spent in a Cincinnati hotel with her husband.

When the hotel manager realized that Dunham was black, he asked her to leave. Naturally, she said no. "Next thing, he sent up a big bruiser," she recalled. "I said, 'What are you here for?' He said he was here to take me bodily out of the room. It was hot, the window was up. So I sat on the sill and put one leg over. I said, 'All right, you come. You come and I will go out this window'—it happened to be high up—'and I have a witness that you pushed me out.' Well, he blanched. Then he turned around and left."

Completing her story, Dunham told an interviewer in 1989, "I like to avoid confrontations if I can. But if I cannot, I want to be totally prepared to solve them or eliminate them, one way or another." Dunham filed lawsuits against the Cincinnati hotel and another in Chicago for refusing to admit blacks.

She eventually won both suits, but bigotry, of course, would not be defeated quickly.

Although Dunham had instructed her manager to avoid bookings in the Deep South, the dancers somehow found themselves playing in segregated theaters. Dunham would have no part of it. Discussing the issue with a biographer, James Haskins, she said, "Usually, as soon as I found out the theater was segregated I would raise such a scandal about it—hold the curtain and do everything possible to make the management uncomfortable—that the management would give in."

Nevertheless, just as *Tropical Review* was about to open in a theater in Louisville, Kentucky, Dunham noticed that all the black patrons were massed in the balcony, whereas the whites enjoyed the orchestra seats. Realizing it was too late to argue, she went on with the show, but at the curtain call, she made her feelings clear.

"Friends," she said to the wildly applauding whites, "we are glad to have made you happy. This is the last time we shall play Louisville because the management refuses to let people like us sit by people like you. Maybe after the war [World War II, which the United States had entered in late 1941] we shall have democracy and I can return. Until then God bless you for you will need it."

This bolt from the blue produced varying reactions. Some people stalked out of the theater, others cheered, and some joined the star backstage. "You shouldn't have done that," chided a white woman. "It was like getting a slap in the face." Dunham snapped back, "How do you think *we* feel?"

Later discussing the incident with a reporter, Dunham said, "The terrific beating the Negro takes must end. You feel you're going to break under the strain. . . . I work with the purpose of reducing the pressure on the Negro performer. In helping him work with a free mind and without stress you help all the Negro people."

Despite such disheartening moments, *Tropical Review* drew enthusiastic audiences everywhere it appeared. In 1943, Dunham brought the show to New York City, which produced the best reception of all. Particularly interesting to critics was the choreographer's new piece, "Rites de Passage," a dance based on African rituals of puberty, fertility, and death.

"Rites" shocked almost everybody, but it also delighted many. Critic John Martin of the *New York Times* wrote, "Certainly it is nothing to take grandma

With partner Roger Ohardieno, Dunham dances in "Barrelhouse," a boisterous crowd pleaser she used in several shows, including 1941's Tropical Review. The choreographer described her "Barrelhouse" character as "a 'beat' old woman who, for a fraction of a Saturday night, becomes young, seductive, and dangerous again."

to see, but it is an excellent piece of work." *Nation* reviewer Virginia Mishnun had reservations, but she admitted that the piece "goes over big with an audience that gets a kick out of sex brought into the parlor by a dancer who is obviously a lady."

So many New Yorkers clamored for tickets to *Tropical Review* that its one-week engagement turned into six. But it fared less well in Boston, a city that traditionally frowned on any but the most innocuous books and shows. Here the local censors took one look at the review and thundered, "No!" Being banned in Boston, however, actually helped business: New Englanders' puritanical attitudes seemed to amuse the rest of the country.

By 1944, when the *Review* tour ended, Dunham decided it was time to take stock of her life. At the age of 35, she was past her prime as a dancer, especially as a dancer whose movements, as one observer put it, "were bigger than life, so full of energy that they threatened to explode from the confines of the stage."

Dunham's wildly abandoned mode of dancing— modern-dance superstar Martha Graham dubbed her the High Priestess of the Pelvic Girdle—was threatened not only by age but by increasingly severe arthritis. Compounded by a buildup of cartilage on both knees, created by years of punishing movements, Dunham's arthritis limited her motions. But it by no means crippled her: She could and would continue to dance. Still, she realized she would have to slow down, at least a little.

Thus far in her career, Dunham had demonstrated her theories, her technique, her choreography with her own body. Now she decided to turn a longtime dream into reality, creating an academy where she could pass these concepts and skills on to a new generation of dancers. In 1945, she opened the Katherine Dunham School of Dance.

At 35, Dunham realized she could not go on dancing forever (although she did, in fact, continue for another 20 years). In 1945, therefore, she opened the Katherine Dunham School of Dance, an institution she hoped would give "the Negro dance-student the courage really to study, and a reason to do so."

Announcing the school's start, Dunham said she would strive "to develop a technique that will be as important to the white man as to the Negro. To attain a status in the dance world that will give to the Negro dance-student the courage really to study, and a reason to do so. And to take *our* dance out of the burlesque—to make it a more dignified art."

Making the school possible was a huge three-story suite of studios, its use donated by millionaire Broadway producer and Dunham admirer Lee Shubert. The school boasted 12 pupils on opening day; 10 months later, enrollment was 420, with a waiting list almost as long.

The dancer, choreographer, and teacher made a characteristically broad choice of students: An equal blend of sexes, half were children, half adults of all ages. One-third of the enrollment was white, the remainder black or of mixed racial and ethnic backgrounds. Pupils came from all over the United States as well as from Europe, Africa, and the Caribbean. Although she was operating on a shoestring, Dunham allowed a large proportion of the students to pay their way by cleaning the studios, mending costumes, or running the elevator.

In its 10-year existence, the Dunham School—America's first predominantly black dance academy—trained an entire generation of black dancers, including entertainer Eartha Kitt and choreographer Arthur Mitchell, future director of the Dance Theatre of Harlem. The school's roster also included such actors as Marlon Brando, Jennifer Jones, and José Ferrer, who came to Dunham to learn body movement.

Along with classes in Dunham's own brand of dance technique, the school offered music, stagecraft, philosophy, anthropology, and foreign languages; "a well-rounded performer should be a well-rounded person," insisted Dunham. So impressive was the school's curriculum, in fact, that Columbia and New York universities accepted work completed at the Dunham School as exchange credits. Almost every Sunday, the school held open rehearsals, which eventually turned into a combination of recital, anthropology lecture, and ebullient party. Actors, ballet stars, politicians, and society figures crammed the studios, often mixing with ambassadors and even presidents from Caribbean, South American, and African nations.

Her school in full swing, the tireless Dunham turned her attention to new ventures. With her company, she made a record album of West Indian music, performed in a television special, and appeared in nightclubs from New York to Las Vegas. In 1946, she completed and published *Journey to Accompong*, an account of her travels in Jamaica. Later that year, the army released Private John Pratt (World War II had ended with Allied victory a year earlier), ready and eager to get back to work. Together, he and his wife put together a new show, *Bal Nègre*, with Pratt as costume and set designer and Dunham as choreographer and dancer.

Bal Nègre, scheduled to run for a month, opened in late 1946 and ran for nine weeks. The review, a mixture of black dance styles from the Caribbean, Africa, Latin America, and the United States, included Dunham's celebrated "L'Ag'Ya," a Voodoo ritual entitled "Majumba," a Brazilian rhumba, a frenzied snake-possession number called "Shango," and several American ragtime dances.

The critics loved it. The theater's "usually staid stage," said one reviewer of *Bal Nègre*, "was alive with glistening, pulsating bodies." Some critics called it "arresting" and "exciting"; another said it "surpasses its predecessors to be far and away the best of the Dunham shows to date." The *New York Times* congratulated Dunham for displaying "a new dignity" and Pratt for creating a show that was "brightly staged and brilliantly costumed."

Glowing with triumph, Dunham turned to yet another frontier, this time arranging her first international tour. In the next two years, she would captivate audiences in Europe, South America, and Mexico. ◖◗

6

NEW WORLDS

Dunham spends a quiet backstage moment during the run of Bal Nègre, *the review she brought to Mexico in 1948. The Illinois dancer quickly conquered the Mexicans, who dubbed her "La Katerina" and mobbed her performances for six months.*

Bal Nègre Brought Katherine Dunham's company not only glowing reviews but more work, this time in Mexico. Offered a four-week booking, the choreographer, who had never traveled beyond the United States and the Caribbean, accepted quickly.

The dancers arrived in Mexico City just in time for their scheduled performance but several days ahead of their costumes and sets, which had been shipped separately. Obeying the first law of the theater—"the show must go on"—the company made its Mexican debut in rehearsal tights, dancing on a bare stage. Members of Mexico's upper class, known for their highly formal manners, belied their reputation on this evening; ignoring the dancers' makeshift presentation, the bejeweled theatergoers cheered themselves hoarse and demanded encore after encore.

Dancing with her trademark cigar, hip-hugging skirts, and manic energy, Dunham—"La Katerina" to her hosts—won the heart of Mexico. As the weeks turned to months of sell-out shows, the American performer found time to delve into anthropological research; the result: "Veracruzana" and other new dances based on Mexican folk traditions.

By now a Mexican national celebrity, Dunham found herself flooded by invitations to lecture on anthropology, appear at balls in her honor, and visit such luminaries as artist Diego Rivera and Mexican president Miguel Alemán. "La Katerina," as a New York newspaper observed, "has certainly rung the bell south of the border." Dunham responded to the acclaim modestly, telling reporters that she hoped her troupe could do more than simply entertain. "Anything that helps explain one group of human beings to another," she said, "will tend to dissipate misunderstandings, fears, and prejudices."

In June 1948, six months after their engagement began, the Dunham Dancers left Mexico for Europe, where history repeated itself: Performing in a review called *Caribbean Rhapsody* in London, the American troupe bowled over the British just as they had the Mexicans. "This daughter of slaves," raved one English ballet critic, "has come as a conqueror to Europe." Said another, "The unity and beauty of [Dunham's] stage ensembles make some of our own ballet productions look more than a little primitive."

The story was the same in France, but with typically exuberant Gallic touches. Parisian dress designers rushed to copy the "Dunham Look"; sculptors created statues of the dancer's feet; a major Paris museum exhibited paintings of the entire company. Referring to the great black entertainer who took the city by storm in the 1920s, the press called Dunham "the most extravagantly successful dancer since Josephine Baker." The attention was flattering but exhausting. "It is nice to be liked," Dunham told a friend, "but in Paris the people devour you!"

Also fatiguing was the job of simultaneously managing the Dunham Dance Company in Europe and the Dunham dance school in New York. Without Dunham's actual presence, enrollment at the school had dropped off, requiring its founder to send her own

money to keep classes going. And to keep the European tour running smoothly, she had to function as more than choreographer and dancer; overseeing a flock of young, high-strung, often extravagant and not always practical dancers, she also served as counselor, housemother, financial watchdog, publicist, travel director, and business manager.

Dunham, already veering between elation over the company's success and what she called "discouragement, doubt, and anxiety," was devastated by the news she received in the spring of 1949: Her beloved brother had died of tuberculosis at the age of 44. Barely able to believe that Albert's "goodness and intellectual brilliance" were no more, she hastened home for his funeral. After giving what comfort

After a triumphant 1948 visit to England, Dunham (center) and her troupe arrive in France. As the "Dunham Look" swept Paris, the dancer found herself surrounded by clothes designers, society hostesses, sculptors, and reporters; "In Paris," she complained gently, "the people devour you!"

she could to her stepmother and father—who would himself be dead before the end of the year—Dunham rejoined her company in Europe.

Except for ordinarily liberal Sweden, where critics accused Dunham of promoting "indecency" and blasted "L'Ag'Ya" as "the most unconcealed erotic exhibition ever performed," the rest of the trip went well. Germany, Belgium, the Netherlands, and Italy passed in a blur of theaters, lights, trains, quarrels, reconciliations, bouquets, and seemingly endless applause.

The Dunham Dance Company returned to New York in a blaze of glory. *Caribbean Rhapsody*, which the troupe introduced to American audiences in 1950, met with almost universal approval. A few critics scolded Dunham for losing her "spontaneity" and becoming too "sophisticated," but most thought she was better than ever.

"Paris has done wonders" for the troupe, said one Manhattan reviewer. "The new Miss Dunham is an assured and lovely artist, possessed of an aristocratic languor which is quite irresistible," wrote another. Pratt, too, earned good words: His costumes, observed the *New York Times*, "contribute one of the most constantly rewarding aspects of Miss Dunham's production."

After its triumphant New York run, the company headed south, spending several months in Brazil, Argentina, and Jamaica. The Latin American swing ended in Haiti, where Dunham and Pratt had leased a huge old villa called Habitation Leclerq. The place was run-down and said to be haunted, but the grounds abounded with lush flowers and trees, statues, fountains and pools, and Dunham adored it. Looking forward to a long, restful vacation, the exhausted choreographer invited her dancers, musicians, stagehands, and widowed stepmother to her new home. Here she breathed a sigh of contentment.

After witnessing the marriage of one of her dancers to a Swiss engineer (left), Dunham signs the registry in a Paris city hall. Foreign tours required the star to act not only as dancer and choreographer but as housemother, banker, travel agent, and publicity director.

That mood did not last long. The first sign of trouble came with the dancers, most of whom missed the bright lights and big cities of their tours. Finding rural Haiti boring, the young artists spent most of their time squabbling and complaining. Annette Dunham, too, failed to appreciate her daughter's adopted land. The people, she said, were too free in their manners and speech; besides, there were no television programs, no church social parties, no group of friends ready for a cup of tea and a chat. To make matters worse, poor Annette claimed to have seen a ghost soon after her arrival.

Alerted by a bloodcurdling shriek one night, Dunham and Pratt rushed to Annette's bedroom, where the shaken woman said a strange black man had awakened her. Sobbing and pleading for help, the man, who was bleeding, bare chested, and had his hands tied behind him, fled through the flower beds when she screamed. Indicating his route, Annette— who had never heard the local ghost stories—pointed in the direction of the villa's old slave quarters.

Pratt and his wife carefully examined the area, but they could find no footprints, no broken flowers, no evidence that anyone had been near Annette's room. The man *had been there*, insisted the distraught stepmother. At this point, Dunham started thinking about the cruel French governor of Haiti who, two centuries earlier, had tortured and killed scores of slaves at the villa Leclerq. The spirits of those unfortunate people, said the locals, continued to wander the land, searching for their murderer.

The next day, Dunham sent for Kam, a very old Voodoo priestess said to be gifted at exorcism, the chasing away of unwelcome spirits. Kam spent a week studying Habitation Leclerq, then proceeded with the ceremonies that, she said, would put the ghosts to rest. Whatever else she did, she provided immense relief to Dunham and her stepmother, who felt a new

Pratt and Dunham relax on the deck of their Haitian home, Habitation Leclerq. Dunham, who adored Haiti, immersed herself in the country's customs and traditions, including the practice of its national religion, Vodun, or Voodoo.

sense of tranquillity, and apparently to the ghost, who was seen no more.

Dunham had undergone the first step of Voodoo initiation (that of the *hounci lavé tête*) in 1936, and she took part in increasingly advanced rites over the years. In the late 1970s, she became a *hounci canzo*, described by experts as "a servitor of the gods who . . . during a hypnotic state called 'possession,' is capable of extreme exposure to heat without showing visible signs of injury." Next, Dunham began the complex process of becoming a *mambo*, or priestess.

As a devout practitioner of Voodoo, Dunham naturally accepted its array of African-rooted gods. She considered herself a daughter of Yemanja, the virgin goddess who bears some resemblance to the Christian Virgin Mary; she also believed herself to be the wife of Damballa, the snake god who rules the universe. Other spiritual figures important to Dunham were Legba, who guards gates and crossroads and may be compared with the Christian St. Peter; and San Lazaro, whose sphere of influence is crippled joints and who was especially significant to the dancer because of her arthritic knees.

In her biography of Dunham, dancer Ruth Beckford explained her friend's attitude toward Yemanja, her chosen "mother" and protector. "Yemanja has an obligation toward Dunham over and beyond that which she owes an ordinary person," she says. "In return, Dunham has obligations she must meet to appease and show gratitude to the virgin. . . . If Yemanja is rightly served, she will always see to it that problems are solved. Just as people offer Christian prayers, Dunham asks of Yemanja, 'Look, I'm your legitimate daughter—you owe me this. Now see to it.' Her requests to Yemanja have for her the same benefits as prayers for people who pray."

During the 1960s, Dunham learned that some of her black neighbors called her "the black witch" because of her ceramic images of Yemanja and other black Voodoo gods. "Well, you know, they are afraid to come [to your house]," a member of the community told the dancer, "because you practice black magic; when they see that black virgin, they are frightened."

Dunham was bemused by such reactions. "Why, in the midst of the black power struggle," she asked herself, "would people feel threatened by a black virgin? Since they accepted all the white spiritual figures in church, such as the Virgin Mary and Christ, their refusal to accept a black spiritual figure was a mystery."

As a youngster, Dunham had attended the African Methodist Episcopal church. Beckford points out, however, that "her parents overlooked the official aspect of having her christened or baptized. Therefore, when viewing it from the standpoint of a lay [nonclerical] person, Dunham probably feels she *is* a witch." Dunham, of course, never worried about being conventional. The prospect of being considered a witch—or even of *being* one—probably never disturbed her in the slightest. ❦

CHALLENGES

AFTER 13 YEARS of marriage, Katherine Dunham, 43, and John Pratt, 39, became parents for the first time. Their new family member, adopted in 1952, was Marie Christine ("M.C.") Columbier, a 5-year-old orphan from the Caribbean island of Martinique.

The couple took their daughter wherever they went, establishing a temporary nursery in each new theater dressing room. M.C. began to imitate her mother from the start, and by the time she was six, she could skillfully apply stage makeup, arrange elaborate headdresses, and sing most of the tunes she heard on stage. When she was old enough, her parents would send her to school in Switzerland; in the meantime, she lived out of a trunk just as the other troupers did.

In 1953, M.C. and her parents departed for their second tour of Europe. The company was about to open in Rome, Italy, when Dunham got a letter from her New York business adviser. Writing about her dance school "and its various problems," the adviser said, "It is costing you somewhere around $800

Marie Christine ("M.C."), the little girl Dunham and Pratt adopted in 1952, prepares to leave on a tour with her parents. M.C. loved to imitate her mother, but she would decide against a career as a dancer, eventually settling in Rome as a guitarist and dance teacher.

Executing one of her last high kicks, a 43-year-old Dunham rehearses for a cakewalk number with partner Vanoye Aikens in London in 1952. By 1955, even the dancer's most fervent admirers would note that although she still exerted "quite irresistible charm," her days of wild gymnastics were over.

weekly, money which would be far more useful in clearing obligations. . . . I see no way to justify it."

The choreographer knew the school was losing money, but until now, she had not realized how bad things were. "It should be closed," said the adviser flatly. Dunham fought the proposal, desperately looking for ways to refloat the sinking ship, but she finally admitted defeat. "Heartsick," as she put it, she shut the school down in 1954.

For Dunham, the end of her cherished school kicked off a spell of bad luck, bad timing, and bad temper. Although surgery on both knees had relieved some of her constant pain, her days of wild gyrations and high kicks were over. Reviewing her 1955 New York City production *Carnaval*, even dance critic Walter Terry, a longtime Dunham admirer, commented on her limited movements. The dancer continued "to exert her quite irresistible charm," said Terry, but "without exerting herself muscularly. Indeed, she rarely indulged in anything more than a hip-swaying shuffle, a mild kick or two, perhaps a backbend." Terry noted that Dunham's magnetism could still "make you forget that anyone else is on stage," but no dance fan could read the review and fail to understand that Dunham's youth had fled.

Following the run of *Carnaval*, the Dunham Dancers took off on an extended tour of Australia and the Far East. This time, the choreographer left her daughter in the United States, sending her to live with her grandmother and attend a regular school in Joliet. At this point, Dunham was feeling less than fit and still smarting over the reception of her last effort. She was also having trouble paying expenses and salaries of her 50-person troupe, and she was unhappy about the lack of government support. As representatives of their nation, other American dance groups received federal subsidies; those companies, Dunham noted angrily, were uniformly white.

"Even some of the more educated Europeans are astounded to find that there is educational oportunity in America for the Negro," she fumed. "I'd like to offset some of that false propaganda." Despite a number of appeals, however, the government never offered Dunham assistance of any kind.

Faced with this array of pains and irritations, Dunham grew increasingly hard to get along with. Australian reporters wrote about how she made dressing-room visitors remove their shoes, kept people waiting with no apology, "dragged her mink coat around as if it were an old rag," and treated everyone on her staff—including her husband—"tyrannically." Katherine Dunham, observed one newspaperwoman tersely, is "a law unto herself."

Like many temperamental people, Dunham seemed to be hardest on those she loved best. And Pratt, affectionate and easygoing though he was, had limits. He took as many tongue-lashings as he could, then, in late 1956, packed his bag and boarded a flight back to Haiti.

Technically only the troupe's set and costume designer, Pratt had actually managed liaisons with local theaters, publicity, plane and train reservations, room and board, medical care, and a thousand other matters essential to the survival of a road company. Now all that fell to Dunham, already overextended by her own responsibilities. Nevertheless, she gritted her teeth and went on with the Asian tour, shepherding her troupe through engagements in Singapore, Hong Kong, the Philippines, and Japan.

The company continued to receive high praise from press and public. But the dancers' spirits, dampened by intense heat, bouts of food poisoning, and Dunham's unpredictable behavior, began to flag. For her part, Dunham was worn out, lonely for her husband and daughter, and deeply concerned about her stepmother, whose health had begun to deteriorate rapidly. Then, in the fall of 1957, just as the company finished its Asian tour, Dunham learned that Annette Dunham had died. Now the dancer hit an all-time low point.

Ending her company's 20-year-existence, she sent the dancers and crew home. Despite the problems that had recently bedeviled them, troupe members felt an enduring loyalty to their leader; the parting was tearful, laced with promises of a reunion in the not-too-distant future. Meanwhile, Dunham decided to stay in Japan and take stock of her life.

Pratt, who had made up the quarrel with his wife by long-distance letters and phone calls, had been with his mother-in-law during her last weeks and had kept his wife informed. After Annette's death, he took M.C. to Habitation Leclerq in Haiti; knowing that her loved ones were safe and in each other's company, Dunham felt able to concentrate on herself for a while. For years, admirers had urged her to write an autobiography; now on her own in Japan, she resolved to try.

After producing an outline and notes for the projected book, Dunham sent them to a literary agent in New York City. Publishers, the agent soon reported, showed great interest in a Dunham autobiography, but their ideas about the project were miles apart from Dunham's. The book, said the publishers, should concentrate on the choreographer's love life, on anecdotes about the celebrities she knew, and on gossip about her colleagues in the dance world.

Dunham wanted to write a simple account about her childhood and adolescence. Her subject, she said, was a woman—herself—who was "made up of some kind of earth as well as star material." Such a work, responded the publishers, had no hope of serious sales. It also had no hope of producing a large financial advance, which Dunham had counted on. Out of

Author Dunham completes her autobiography, A Touch of Innocence, *at Habitation Leclerq in 1958. Published the following year, the book earned glowing reviews: "One of the most extraordinary life stories I have ever read," said a* New York Times *critic.*

money, she temporarily shelved her writing and accepted a Hollywood offer to choreograph a new film, *Green Mansions.* In the summer of 1958, she returned to the United States.

Dunham dutifully fulfilled her movie commitment, but she spent every free moment pounding out her book. Her new sample chapters brought a positive response: A prominent New York publisher, Harcourt Brace, offered to sign a contract if she would agree to make certain revisions. More than willing to make them, she finshed her work in Hollywood and rejoined her husband and daughter in Haiti.

Writing almost nonstop, Dunham completed what she called "the story of the first painful 18 years of my life" and sent it off to New York. On target, said Harcourt Brace, which scheduled *A Touch of Innocence* for publication in the fall of 1959.

The memoir scored a hit. A typical review came from the *New York Times* critic, who described it as "one of the most extraordinary life stories I have ever read." In *A Touch of Innocence*, continued the *Times* reviewer, "not one breath of sentimentality or self-pity mars or falsifies the clear picture of [Dunham's] girlhood, her family, or her surroundings. This story of a childhood and youth becomes a mature exploration of the human spirit, its perils, and its dignities."

Successful as it was, Dunham's autobiography did not make her rich; in order to maintain Habitation Leclerq, she needed to generate a steady income. The answer, she decided, was to turn the place into a luxury resort that would attract wealthy vacationers from the United States and Europe. Accordingly, she and her husband began constructing guest cottages, a Japanese-style bar, an African-theme nightclub, a small zoo, and other amenities for the hordes of visitors they hoped to entertain.

Completing the new facility in 1961, the hopeful hoteliers sent out brochures, gave interviews to travel writers, and launched an international advertising campaign. The project, however, never got off the ground. The first strike against it came before the opening, when a pair of African snakes managed to escape the hotel zoo. Almost instantly, a wave of false but fearsome rumors swept the Haitian countryside. From two, the number of serpents spread to a dozen, then hundreds. Radio stations shrilled with warnings about the marauders, said to be slithering through the land, devouring not only children but grown men and even donkeys.

The furor caught the attention of President François Duvalier and his dictatorial government, which suggested that the snakes posed a threat to national security. Squads of Duvalier's secret police, the dreaded *Tonton Macoutes*, began skulking around Habitation Leclerq, unnerving the executives and scaring off many local workers. Finally, instead of closing the hotel, Duvalier merely ordered the rest of the hotel's snakes confiscated. The move relieved Dunham and her husband, but it did not help their enterprise.

What really doomed it was politics and poverty: Understandably, few tourists wanted to fend off crowds of ragged beggars or stroll through acres of wretched, reeking slums. Fewer still sought relaxation in a land controlled by an all-powerful dictator and his terrifying, black-clad private police force. As Duvalier's international reputation worsened, foreign visitors steered increasingly clear of Haiti, wiping out such projects as the Leclerq resort. Dunham still loved Haiti, but she realized she would have to make her living elsewhere.

In 1962, a solution suggested itself: Stephen Papich, a Hollywood producer and former Dunham dance student, asked her to put together a new Broadway review. Papich, who pointed out Dunham's long absence from the American stage, said he was willing, able, and eager to back her in a comeback. Not surprisingly, Dunham responded with an emphatic "Yes!"

Assembling their cast, Dunham, Pratt, and Papich made a sweeping tour of western Africa, auditioning and hiring dancers and musicians as they went. Returning with 25 authentic tribal performers and a handful of old Dunham regulars, the choreographer put together a show she called *Bamboche* (get-together, in Haitian dialect). Once again, Pratt designed the production. And once again, critics greeted their work with delight. "Gorgeously staged," said one. "A slick combination of blatant showmanship and honest-to-goodness folklore," trumpeted another.

The 51-year-old Dunham, who had added excess weight to her other physical problems, earned raves nonetheless. She looked "as lithe and subtle and sexy in her abbreviated costumes as a woman decades

Arriving at New York City's international airport in 1962, a Moroccan dancer performs an impromptu number with Dunham. The choreographer had brought the young man to America as one of the stars in Bamboche, *a new review in which she also appeared.*

younger," said one observer. Another wrote, "The youngsters will learn from the lady herself what she means about 'spirit' in the Dunham way of dance, in this particular case a lowdown bezazz that technique alone cannot muster."

Shortly after *Bamboche* opened, however, New York fell into the grip of a citywide newspaper strike, eliminating any chance of publicizing the musical's glittering reviews. Faced with a large, expensive cast and virtually no ticket sales, Papich had to close the show, which Dunham had called "my best work."

Disappointed but even now undiscouraged, Dunham quickly found a new outlet for her gifts. When

Dunham, the first black choreographer to work for New York City's Metropolitan Opera Company, rehearses her dancers for the Met's 1962 production of Aïda. Infusing the drama—which takes place in ancient Egypt—with Voodoo rhythms and West African tribal dances, Dunham evoked screams of outrage from the staid opera world.

Manhattan's Metropolitan Opera Company invited her to choreograph its new production of the great Giuseppe Verdi work *Aïda*, she accepted at once, although she had no previous experience whatsoever with the medium. *Aïda*, set in ancient Egypt, inspired Dunham to use African-based dance patterns and to season them with a touch of Voodoo-style rhythms.

The result horrified most opera reviewers. Dunham, they said, failed to understand the composer's goals and had distracted attention from the music by employing irrelevant themes. Her dances, one critic sniffed, were "dandy for Voodoo but not for Verdi." But one of the somewhat stuffy experts defended Dunham. "Taken together," said the Dunham supporter, "ancient Egypt, 19th-century Italian music, and the conventions of operatic spectacle are simply incompatible with any style of dancing known to man. . . . Blame the Metropolitan, therefore, if you don't like the Dunham dances, but don't blame her. She has not changed her stripes, she has not stinted on her efforts, and she has not shortchanged the management."

Dunham's *Aïda* choreography created more than one admirer. Southern Illinois University (SIU) executives had been searching for the right person to serve as artist-in-residence and to stage a brand-new production of composer Charles Gounod's 1859 opera *Faust*. As soon as they saw the Metropolitan's controversial *Aïda*, they knew they had found their woman: They offered the post to Dunham.

Always unable to resist a challenge, she signed on and, with her husband, relocated in Carbondale, Illinois. Fate finally began to smile again: Dunham's return to the Midwest would usher in one of the most satisfying periods of her creative life. ✸

8

STEALING THE SHOW

❧

KATHERINE DUNHAM SET her 1965 production of *Faust*, originally a medieval legend, in the Germany of the 1930s. This innovative approach sharpened the focus on Faust, who sold his soul to the Devil in return for earthly gain, by comparing him with Adolf Hitler, the Nazi dictator who ordered the death of millions in his quest for world domination.

The opera's opening scene, according to a local newspaper, presented an image of "stark horror, with bodies frozen in their action, strung on wires, on stumps of trees, and on the ground." Other Dunham touches included dancers playing basketball with a human skull, a Teutonic striptease artist conducting a child's funeral, and a motorcyclist—the Devil himself—clad in black leather and roaring across the stage to grab Faust's soul. Some purists quaked at Dunham's revolutionary concept, but no one denied its stunning dramatic impact.

SIU officials were so impressed with it, in fact, that they asked Dunham to remain with the university. They also offered her permanent space to house

A Southern Illinois University student listens to Dunham explain her theory of dance technique. It was her work at SIU that introduced the choreographer to East St. Louis, a violent, impoverished community filled with troubled teenagers. Moving there in 1967, she would open the Performance Arts Training Center, a school aimed at assisting minority youth.

95

and display her memorabilia, by this point an immense trove of costumes, manuscripts, letters, pictures, and artifacts from all over the world. Dunham liked the idea. She accepted the title of Visiting Artist in the Fine Arts Division and agreed to store her treasures at the SIU branch in nearby East St. Louis.

Dunham was both shocked and inspired by what she saw in East St. Louis. Situated across the Mississippi River from St. Louis, Missouri, the community had once been a sleepy, largely white ferry station for its sister city. Its riverfront location made it a choice spot for manufacturers, who began to build plants around the turn of the century. Then, during America's participation in World War I (1917–18), when East St. Louis's suddenly booming factories needed a huge supply of workers, the city began to attract large numbers of southern blacks.

The blacks' willingness to work for very low wages enraged lower-class whites, whose fury eventually exploded into one of the most savage racial conflicts in America's history. In July 1917, screaming mobs murdered at least 39 black men, women, and children; injured hundreds more; and torched some 6,000 black homes. After the massacre, whites started abandoning the city; by the mid-1960s, when Dunham arrived there, its population was at least 60 percent black.

Deserted by most of its whites, the bulk of its factories abandoned, plagued by poverty and crime, East St. Louis turned into an ongoing nightmare. Illiteracy was high, unemployment the norm; gangs ruled the streets, riots occurred regularly, bombings and sniper shootings were so common that they barely made the news. With almost no tax base to pay for services, the city allowed its streets, parks, and bridges to crumble, its garbage to go uncollected, its empty buildings to burn unimpeded. For blacks, East

St. Louis had become a metaphor for all that had gone wrong with the American dream.

Not surprisingly, the devastated streets spawned a generation of angry, bitter young people. "I was shocked at the violence, the rage so often turned inward on the community itself," Dunham recalled. "It was so disheartening, all those young men going up in flames." But lack of heart had never troubled Dunham, who decided that she herself would try to improve the empty lives of East St. Louis's restless and unhappy youth.

After researching the situation carefully, she came up with a plan. It revolved around a school, one much like the school she had operated in New York. Along with dance training, it would offer courses in music, African languages and arts, the martial arts, and anthropology. Dunham was preoccupied with dance

Dunham confers with President Léopold Senghor in Dakar, Senegal, in 1962. The African leader had asked the American dancer to advise him on the First World Festival of Negro Arts, an elaborate event he hosted in 1965 and 1966.

as always, but in this case, she saw it as a special tool: "Dance as it would serve the East St. Louis project," she wrote, "is concerned with the fundamentals of human society."

At this point—the turbulent 1960s—the civil rights movement was in full swing, and the government had finally begun to face up to the issue of black needs. Congress was providing money for projects and agencies that would educate and assist minority youths, particularly in the nation's seething urban ghettos. The federal Office of Economic Opportunity (OEO) was one such agency.

Drawing up a proposal for what she entitled the Performing Arts Training Center (PATC), Dunham submitted it to the OEO in the spring of 1965. For additional funding, she also applied to the university and to an assortment of foundations. "East St. Louis has been the focal point of racial resentments, riots, delinquency, and poverty for many years," she wrote. "The need for objectives to replace crime and delinquency, for disciplines for the leisure time of the young . . . are grave preoccupations."

Meanwhile, Dunham had received a number of work offers, projects that would bring in added revenue as well as provide employment for former members of her dance troupe. Because federal agencies and private foundations tend to move at a glacially slow pace, she knew she had time; as soon as SIU gave her the freedom to do so, she flew off to Italy.

In Rome, Dunham choreographed the dance sequences for *The Bible*, a 20th Century Fox film starring Ava Gardner and George C. Scott, as well as the dances for a Marcello Mastroianni stage production. From Rome, she went to Paris to choreograph another show, then flew to New York, where she rounded up almost all of the old Dunham Dance

Company and staged a performance for the American Ballet Theatre's 25th anniversary celebration.

Not even winded, the 56-year-old choreographer next flew to Africa, where she had been invited to train the National Ballet of Senegal. The official guest of Senegal's president Léopold Senghor, Dunham also agreed to act as his adviser on the First World Festival of Negro Arts, to be held in Senegal in 1965 and 1966.

She experienced a touch of cultural trouble in the African republic: the Senegalese ballet dancers wanted her to help them develop European and American dance styles; Dunham insisted that as members of their nation's official national troupe, they should re-create their own dance heritage, not imitate others. The American choreographer thus found herself in the unique position of telling Africans how to be African.

Such apparent contradictions had never bothered Dunham before, and they did not bother her now. When the arts festival opened, she smiled serenely as the Senegalese National Ballet performed a series of Senegalese dances, accompanied by Senegalese music—and thunderous applause from a distinguished international audience.

In the slivers of time she could snatch between performances, classes, movies, stage shows, and conferences, Dunham worked on a book about Haiti, *Island Possessed*. Published in 1969, it earned good marks from reviewers, who described Dunham's love affair with her adopted country as "frank" and "fascinating."

Although it openly called him a "tyrant," the book pleased even Haitian president François Duvalier, who said it presented "the true personality of the nation and the Haitian people." Dunham herself called *Island Possessed* "a book written with love, dedicated to my husband, John Pratt, and to the Republic of Haiti explaining, I think, many things about this author and that island."

With Pratt, Dunham returned to East St. Louis in 1967, the year that the OEO finally granted her the money for a training center. She also received financial pledges from SIU and from the Rockefeller Foundation, which had offered to fund her anthropological studies so many years earlier.

Dunham started her new venture with a bang. Soon after she announced her plan to reach out to the young people of East St. Louis, members of the Imperial Warlords, a prominent local gang, asked her to meet with them in a local bar. (Although they sneered at dancing, the Warlords were impressed with Dunham's firsthand knowledge of Africa and intrigued by her promise of classes in percussion and martial arts.)

After a surprisingly cordial meeting with the teenagers, Dunham headed for her car, accompanied by her 19-year-old daughter, M.C., and two of the boys from the gang. Later recalling the evening—a typical one for East St. Louis—Dunham said, "The city was burning—the sky was red with fires left and right. There were police cars, sirens, stoplights, headlights." Suddenly, a patrol car pulled up. Police officers stepped out, grabbed the young men, and threw them inside.

Dunham demanded to know what was going on. "None of your business," snapped an officer. The squad car roared off. Dunham sent M.C. home, then sped to the police station. Finding her young friends waiting to be booked, Dunham asked for an explanation. "There's a fire in town," replied one of the Warlords. "They pick up all the young people they can; they don't ask questions."

Approaching "a big, tough-looking Irish cop," Dunham said the Warlords must have legal representation. "Lady, you shut up if you know what's good for you," he responded. That was all Dunham needed. After giving the Irish officer a piece of her mind, she turned to two black policemen. "You certainly ought to be ashamed of the way you earn your living," she said scathingly. Next, she marched up to the sergeant's desk and shouted, "All right, if you want to arrest somebody, arrest me!"

"You get out of here!" roared the sergeant. Dunham stood her ground. "So he shoved me," she said, "and I shoved back at this great, huge hunk of Irish flesh and muscle. It was like shoving against a brick wall. Then two other big cops started twisting my arms. I asked if I were under arrest and they said, 'You sure are!'"

In the end, the policemen dragged Dunham off to a jail cell, where she spent the night, booked on charges of disorderly conduct. M.C. and her father arrived on the scene early the next morning.

Senator Adlai Stevenson of Illinois meets in his Washington, D.C., office with Dunham and some of her young friends from East St. Louis. Supervised by the choreographer, the youngsters later performed at the 1970 White House Conference on Children. "We stole the show," Dunham chortled later.

After receiving medals for their contributions to the performing arts, Dunham and the other 1983 winners of the Kennedy Center Honors gather in the nation's capital. At Dunham's right sits actor James Stewart; standing, left to right, are film director Elia Kazan, composer Virgil Thomson, and entertainer Frank Sinatra.

Chagrined to discover they had arrested an international celebrity, the police released their prisoner and dropped the charges. Soon afterward, the embarrassed mayor of East St. Louis presented Dunham with the key to the city.

But it was Dunham's arrest, not the key, that opened doors for her in East St. Louis. She could probably have found no better way to reach her targets than by getting herself arrested while defending a pair of Warlords. "This was a tough lady," said one new admirer.

By twos and threes, wary but curious teenagers started coming around the new Performance Arts Training Center. Finding a staff of friendly, unpatronizing teachers, many of them young themselves—a number of Dunham's former students had elected to join her at the school—the East St. Louis youngsters slowly lost their distrust.

Within a few months, classes had begun to fill. Even the toughest of the boys enrolled. They started with subjects that interested them, such as karate, but soon branched out, some of them studying Japanese with the martial arts instructor, some taking lessons in percussion, others even venturing into drama and dance groups. Following the lead of their older brothers and sisters, the area's younger children gradually made their own appearance.

The success of PATC was uneven but constant. Such a project, of course, could not transform East St. Louis into a model city, but it could and did begin to shed some light into corners long dark and neglected. Dunham's growing number of supporters swelled with pride, for example, when she was invited to the 1970 White House Conference on Children. She accepted on condition that she could bring a group of her East St. Louis youngsters along with her to Washington.

Dunham appeared in the nation's capital with a troupe of 43 children. "It was a hair-raising experience in some ways," she recalled with amusement. "To get ready for an onstage rehearsal there in Washington, we had to round up all those wild little boys in the halls of the hotels." Then she added with characteristic assurance, "Of course, we stole the show."

Interviewed about her plans for PATC, Dunham had once explained: "What we are trying to do is break through apathy. It's not so much teaching people to perform as it is teaching them, through performing, that they have individual worth and can relate to other people."

Many years later, one of her former East St. Louis students suggested that Dunham had accomplished her goal. "I think if you really take her message," said dance instructor Glory Van Scott in the early 1980s, "you will turn around and take the ball and go with

With Vanoye Aikens, her dance partner from 1943 to 1963, Dunham holds a 1987 press conference in New York City. The dancers told reporters they were recreating some of Dunham's most celebrated dances for The Magic of Katherine Dunham, *a presentation by the Alvin Ailey American Dance Theater scheduled to open in Manhattan, then tour the nation.*

it. You realize you are a worthwhile person, that your perimeter is not just where you live, that you can find a wider range."

Dunham's achievements have been recognized not only by her students but by foundations, universities, dance associations, and cultural centers. In 1980, she was the subject of the widely viewed "Divine Drumbeats: Katherine Dunham and Her People," an episode of television's prestigious "Dance in America" series. Among her many accolades are the 1979 Albert Schweitzer Music Award, the 1983 Kennedy Center Honors, an honorary doctor of laws degree from Lincoln University in 1984, and the Scripps American Dance Festival Award in 1986.

At the time of the Schweitzer Award, *New York Times* critic Clive Barnes said, "What can one say about Katherine Dunham? That this woman revolutionized American dance." Other celebrants credited Dunham with paving the way for such renowned companies as Arthur Mitchell's Dance Theatre of Harlem and the Alvin Ailey American Dance Theater. Dance scholar Arthur Todd said, she "put Negro dancing on the map once and for all."

The 1980s produced grief as well as triumph for Dunham. John Pratt, her husband of 47 years, died in early 1986. And her East St. Louis venture, like many of the nation's cultural institutions, faltered during the decade's hard economic times. Then in 1990 a group of admirers—business executives, dance professionals, Ford Foundation officials, and others—banded together to help the choreographer-teacher continue her work. As a start, they staged a fund-raising gala that produced some $35,000, a sum soon matched by the National Endowment for the Arts.

At the gala, a banquet and performance held in East St. Louis in mid-1991, dance critic Jennifer Dunning watched the Dunham Children's Workshop recital with mounting respect. The young dancers "expertly move through pieces in a wide variety of styles," she observed. "Well-schooled, they dance with a rare expansiveness and joy."

The Dunham children, continued Dunning, are "what the world calls disadvantaged. But each is a member of an elect group. Each is a dancer, moving across the makeshift stage of the workshop with an easy, gracious consciousness of self. That has been the mission of Miss Dunham."

As she presided over the 1991 festivities, the 82-year-old Dunham talked about starting her East St. Louis project: "I was trying to steer them into something more constructive than genocide," she said of the area's youngsters. "Everyone needs, if not a culture hero, a culturally heroic society. There is nothing stronger in a [human being] than the need to grow."

"Dancers came into the company like mice and walked out as straight as cornstalks," added Lucille Ellis, a longtime Dunham dancer and teacher. "Miss D. taught people to be proud of themselves."

Beating time on a tabletop with her fingers, Dunham continued to watch her students intently. "It can be done," she said softly. "Don't tell me no." ◗

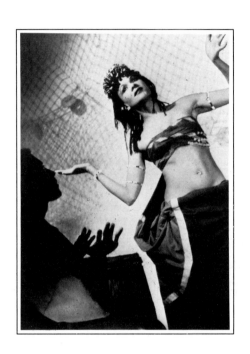

CHRONOLOGY

———— ⟨⟨⟩⟩ ————

1909   Born Katherine Dunham on June 22 in Chicago, Illinois

1924   Stages first show, a church-sponsored musical revue

1928   Enters University of Chicago

1931   Opens dance school in Chicago; stages "Negro Rhapsody"

1935   Receives a Rosenwald Fund fellowship to study African-derived dance patterns in the Caribbean

1936   Becomes initiate of Voodoo religion; receives bachelor's degree from University of Chicago

1939   Marries artist John Pratt; forms Dunham Dance Company

1940   Choreographs and appears in *Tropics and Le Jazz Hot*; collaborates with choreographer George Balanchine on *Cabin in the Sky*, an all-black Broadway musical

1941–44   Stages *Tropical Review* and tours America with it

1945   Opens Katherine Dunham School of Dance in Manhattan

1946   Publishes *Journey to Accompong*, an account of her Caribbean research trip; presents a musical, *Bal Nègre*

1948–50   Tours Mexico and Europe with her dance company; choreographs and stars in *Caribbean Rhapsody*; tours Latin America; acquires a villa in Haiti

1952   Adopts Marie Christine Columbier, a 5-year-old orphan

1955   Stages *Carnaval*; tours Australia and the Far East

1959   Publishes autobiography, *A Touch of Innocence*

1962   Choreographs and makes last Broadway appearance in *Bamboche*; choreographs *Aïda* for New York City's Metropolitan Opera Company

1965   Stages dances for the opera *Faust* at Southern Illinois University (SIU); becomes SIU artist-in-residence; helps run First World Festival of Negro Arts in Dakar, Senegal

1967   Moves to East St. Louis, Illinois; opens Performance Arts Training Center (PATC), a school for impoverished young blacks

1969   Publishes book about Haiti, *Island Possessed*

1979   Receives Albert Schweitzer Music Award, the first of many public honors

1980   Becomes subject of television special "Katherine Dunham and Her People"

1984   Accepts honorary doctorate from Lincoln University

1992   Continues to direct PATC operations in East St. Louis

FURTHER READING

Aschenbrenner, Joyce. *Katherine Dunham*. New York: Congress on Research in Dance, 1981.

Beckford, Ruth. *Katherine Dunham: A Biography*. New York: Dekker, 1979.

Biemiller, Ruth. *Dance: The Story of Katherine Dunham*. New York: Doubleday, 1969.

Buckle, Richard, ed. *Katherine Dunham: Her Dancers, Singers, Musicians*. London: Ballet, 1949.

Coe, Robert. *Dance in America*. New York: Dutton, 1985.

Dunham, Katherine. *Dances of Haiti*. Los Angeles: Center for Afro-American Studies, University of California, Los Angeles, 1983.

———. *Island Possessed*. Garden City, NY: Doubleday, 1969.

———. *Katherine Dunham's Journey to Accompong*. Westport: Negro Universities Press, 1971.

———. *A Touch of Innocence*. New York: Books for Libraries, 1980.

Harnan, Terry. *African Rhythm—American Dance*. New York: Knopf, 1974.

Haskins, James. *Katherine Dunham*. New York: Coward, McCann & Geoghegan, 1982.

Rose, Albirda. *Dunham Technique*. Dubuque: Kendall/Hunt, 1990.

INDEX

PICTURE CREDITS

———— ❦ ————

JEANNINE DOMINY holds a bachelor's degree from Yale University and a master of fine arts degree from Columbia University. She also attended the University of California, Berkeley, and has studied ballet and jazz dancing with the Donna Jansen Ballet Company.

NATHAN IRVIN HUGGINS, one of America's leading scholars in the field of black studies, helped select the titles for the BLACK AMERICANS OF ACHIEVEMENT series, for which he also served as senior consulting editor. He was the W.E.B. Du Bois Professor of History and of Afro-American Studies at Harvard University and the director of the W.E.B. Du Bois Institute for Afro-American Research at Harvard. He received his doctorate from Harvard in 1962 and returned there as a professor in 1980 after teaching at Columbia University, the University of Massachusetts, Lake Forest College, and the California State University, Long Beach. He was the author of four books and dozens of articles, including *Black Odyssey: The Afro-American Ordeal in Slavery*, *The Harlem Renaissance*, and *Slave and Citizen: The Life of Frederick Douglass*, and was associated with the Children's Television Workshop, National Public Radio, the Boston Athenaeum, the Museum of Afro-American History, the Howard Thurman Educational Trust, and Upward Bound. Professor Huggins died in 1989, at the age of 62, in Cambridge, Massachusetts.